MIRACLES
on the
BAYOU

by
Jean Morris Long

ISBN Number: 978-0-692-83691-0

Library of Congress Control Number: 2017932200

Designed by
Gloria C. White & Associates, Memphis, TN

To Mom, Dad, Billy and Bobby,

the Keo community of my childhood

and always my husband Bill,

who has faithfully and patiently seen

the completion of this life-long project.

Table of Contents

Our home on the farm

Preface

Finding Kate, my first published book, chronicled my efforts to learn more about my paternal grandmother, Catherine Lewis Morris. The result was the remarkable story of a remarkable life, told through her letters and my grandfather's diary. Sadly, it was a life cut short by tuberculosis when my father was only ten years old.

But while the end of Kate's life was the end of the book, it was also a part of the circle of life. My father, William Nathan Morris, grew up and came home to the very farmhouse that had welcomed our grandmother as a young bride. My brothers and I lived there as children during the Great Depression, in possibly the "worst of times," but in our memories it was a world of miracles, magic, and dreams, inspired by the quiet heroes whose lives shaped our own.

I did not think of the people around me as being any different from those in the rest of the world, but as the years went by, I found myself writing stories about them. It seemed important for me to record bits and pieces that I remembered through the eyes of a child. From grammar school scribbles in pencil to typewritten attempts in college and now into the computer age, I managed to save every word.

In this book I bring these stories from my childhood all safely together in one place. They are filled with the treasured history of another time and the simple wisdom of ages past. Through these stories, I hope to honor the noble lives that were so important in shaping my own, and to bring them back to life for generations after my own.

In Macrina Wiederkehr's exceptional book of devotions, perceptions, and meditations, *A Tree Full of Angels*, there is a poem called "Is There A Lost Child in You?". An excerpt from this work best expresses why writing this book is so important to me:

> *There are days when*
> *my adult ways*
> *turn tasteless in my mouth*
> *and the child of long ago*
> *starts*
> *pressing on my soul.*
>
> *On days like that*
> *I long to touch that child again*
> *and let her take me by the hand*
> *and lead me down*
> *a path that has a heart*
> *and show me all the things*
> *that*
> *I've stopped seeing*
> *because I've grown too tall.*

A hundred million miracles

A hundred million miracles

Are happ'ning ev'ry day

And those who say

They don't agree

Are those

Who do not hear or see

A hundred million miracles

A hundred million miracles

Are happ'ning ev'ry day.

From the song "A Hundred Million Miracles"
Flower Drum Song

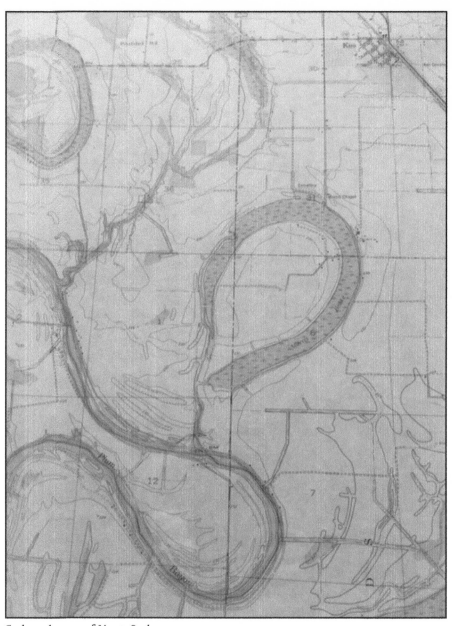

Geological survey of Morris Brake

Prologue

ON THE RIDGE overlooking the bayou known as "The Morris Brake" stood sixteen tenant houses. These weathered gray cypress shacks held families whose grandfathers had served as slaves on this land. The houses where they lived and the fields where they worked bore their names long after they had died or moved to town. The level Arkansas cotton fields suddenly dropped down to a dusty road rimming the swamp-like waters.

Those waters had flowed freely as part of the Arkansas River until 1812, when the famous New Madrid Earthquake struck. To this day it is the most powerful earthquake ever recorded east of the Rockies. The newspaper in Little Rock reported that it "rolled the ground in three foot waves…causing the Mississippi River to run backward, knocked the Arkansas River right out of its bed," and, most famously, created Reelfoot Lake. By cutting off a curving loop of the Arkansas, it formed the low wetlands and the bayou that wound around in front of our house.

Willow trees and bamboo cane hid the dark waters that lay trapped underneath bright green scum and lily pads. In the center of the brake was a large open space where dim light filtered through thick summer foliage. It was cool and quiet inside this mysterious place, with the wide gnarled trunks of cypress tress stretching upward from dark shadows like columns in a great cathedral. Water moccasins slithered down low limbs and disappeared in the black liquid while turtles floated as still as the decaying logs that surrounded them.

The gentle spring breezes that blew through the wooded waters would sometimes build to a frightening roar, sending families down into storm cellars to escape the tornadoes that swept across the flat land. Some said it was the bayou that protected us from their dreaded destruction.

On summer nights, as we children lay in our beds lulled by the steady hum of crickets and frogs, a sudden loud splash would jar our thoughts to the legendary alligator living inside this primeval forest at the foot of our front yard. There was something frightening about the bayou, but it allowed us to be independent and protected us from the rest of the world. Its waters provided catfish and bream, its shade cooled the hot dusty road to town, its trees yielded tough cypress for the walls of our homes and wood to burn in our winter stoves. For a child, it was magic.

The primeval forest at the foot of our yard

MIRACLES
on the
BAYOU

The Farm

MY TWO BROTHERS and I were the fourth generation to grow up on my family's farm and the third generation to live in the farmhouse my grandfather built. Our house sat in the middle of a cotton field. All that separated it from the rows of blooming cotton stalks was a neat lawn and two silver maple trees. We lived two miles outside the small town of Keo, Arkansas, 25 miles southeast of Little Rock.

In the 1930s, rural Arkansas was far behind the level of modernization the rest of the country enjoyed. Before the arrival of Rural Electric of Arkansas and butane gas, Delco batteries powered our lights and we cooked on a wood-burning home range. We did not have a telephone until I was sixteen.

During those economically depressed times, cotton brought only a few cents per pound, but my father clung tenaciously to the land that belonged to his family. Relatives told stories about my great-grandfather, who made the long trek to California to seek his fortune and returned with his gold bounty to buy all of the rich Arkansas River bottomland that his treasure would afford. His acreage was divided among his heirs who further divided it among their children.

When the land was divided between my father and his three siblings, his share included a small white frame house, 700 acres, 16 tenant families, and all of the antiquated traditions of sharecrop farming. He respected the hierarchies and moral codes of this 20th century feudal system, and he had great faith in the instincts of his seasoned tenants. He was the landlord, but he allowed the farm to run on its own natural order, an order established generations before.

Most of the tenants had lived here when he was a child and survived long before he returned from his seven years in the US Navy.

Each tenant was assigned a 15-acre section of land, from which they kept half the yearly profits. They could earn additional income by doing seasonal work such as driving a tractor or picking cotton. At harvest time, my father held his yearly session with each sharecropper in his dusty lint-covered cotton gin office. His earnest counseling on saving and getting ahead often fell on deaf ears, for the fall was a joyous time and a celebration of plenty.

Mule drawn wagons, brimming with cotton, pulled up on the gin scales where their weight was recorded and later payments made at the going rate per pound. The happy recipients felt that the rewards of their labor would last forever. Mattie Brown had gold caps put on her perfectly good teeth, while her husband Buster bought a used car of questionable reliability. But there was always enough cash left to buy new shoes for the children. If a family spent their entire profits during the first few days or lost their money in a crap game, my father "furnished them," carrying them through another year by paying their bills at the general store in town until the next fall.

It was hard to survive the cold winters and lack of conveniences, but there was usually enough, provided one was diligent in planting a garden and cutting firewood from the bayou before bad weather set in. Most took advantage of the land's abundance, but a few less industrious souls who ignored their responsibilities might be found burning their back door steps for warmth.

At the other end of the bayou was a large white clapboard church with a steeple for the tenants who lived on the farm. On its concrete cornerstone our family name was crudely scratched the word "chapel" misspelled: "Morris Chappel, 1904." There, the souls that were replenished each Sunday were sent to heaven in a glorious style. Funerals with burials in a cemetery across the road became day-long celebrations and a rendering to God what was His. A cappella voices rose in the quick natural rhythms of some ancient tribal tradition, but the words expressed Christian joy in this final coming home to Jesus. Each Sunday our family rode past this crowded sanctuary to attend the much smaller white Methodist Church in town.

The town of Keo was also an important part of our lives. Early every morning, my father drove to the post office to get our mail and to pick up the daily newspaper from Little Rock. Downtown Keo consisted primarily of three connected brick stores lined up along Main Street, which was nothing more than a gravel road. The city's only concrete sidewalks were laid in front of Mr. Leake's drugstore, Uncle Jimmie's dry good business, and Mr. French's grocery store. At the free-standing post office next door, Mr. Waller, the postmaster, also sold and repaired radios. A tin roof overhang supported by iron pipe posts provided cover from the rain and summer sun.

Mr. Leake's drugstore has become Charlotte's Restaurant

On Saturdays, everyone from the surrounding farms who came into town crowded underneath its protection to greet friends and visit. Keo boasted a population of 200. The local physician was an "eclectic doctor," meaning that he had not actually finished his medical degree. There was a soda fountain in the drugstore, something not every small town had. There were also two gas stations, two cotton gins, and two schoolhouses, but not because the population demanded it. One was for Blacks and the other for Whites.

In the spring, at 4:30 a.m., the rusty iron bell on the roof of the smokehouse behind our home summoned the workers to headquarters each day. It was Buster who gave the men who gathered around the barn their instructions. When my father returned from the Navy with little knowledge of farming, Buster quietly directed his education, based on years of experience and having lived through seasons of good and bad crops. He had an uncanny knowledge of which field was best suited for cotton, soybeans, or rice. My father said Buster was a genius with computation because he could keep in his head the daily figures for cotton picking and chopping. It was he who paid each workman in cash with proven precision. He had long ago earned complete trust in his mathematical figures and planting decisions. During a summer drought, he was in charge of the system of irrigation ditches with the firm conviction that "If you don't keep ahead of it, it'll get ahead of you!" He and my father had a deep mutual respect.

Walter Bell had a horse saddled up and ready each morning for my father's daily ride around the farm. Walter had "a gift" with animals and was solely responsible for the important task of pairing the mule teams that ploughed the fields. When the first John Deere tractor (with iron lug wheels) was purchased, Aaron Murray became the main tractor driver, a position that carried a certain power and authority. James Taylor was the blacksmith. The carpenter was called "Big Un" for his immense size—to this day I don't know his actual name. Henry Harris was another tractor driver and mechanic. Each man had a crucial role to play on the farm, and each took pride in his singular position.

This isolated society remained independent from the world beyond the bayou. Adeline was the midwife to deliver all of the babies born on the farm. It was said that she practiced voodoo in her cypress shack close by the mossy waters.

Widows like Roxie remained in their homes long after their husbands were gone. She could pick more cotton than any other worker, and no one questioned her ability to carry an equal load. The men helped plow her allotment after they finished their own acreage. Someone always showed up to chop her wood. This unique community always took care of its own and overseeing it all was my father.

My Father

MY FATHER BELIEVED in miracles. Living on the land meant relying totally on the whims of nature for survival. He trusted in the grace of the Lord and in his own "sixth sense," which he claimed you had to have if you were going to be a decent farmer. The consequences of the few times that he failed to outguess the weather were met with quiet acceptance. A crop failure was never permanent. Every spring there would be a new beginning. The dead brown cotton stalks were ploughed under, fresh rows laid and new seed planted. That was when my father awaited the miracle, sometimes impatiently. I remember watching him get down from his horse and kick the dirt with his boot to find a tiny green sprout underneath the hard crust.

My Dad was not a large man. On workdays he wore khaki pants, a freshly ironed shirt, and Wellington boots which he could easily slip off at the back door if they happened to be muddy. A safari-like "pith helmet" protected his face from the unrelenting sun. There was a genteel quality about him that was unique in this rather rough Arkansas frontier land of the early 1930s.

He lost his mother when he was only ten years old. Although the children were young, Kate Morris had already instilled in them a proud sense of family, stern Episcopal principles and a deep obligation to their fellow man. He attended the rambling old schoolhouse in Keo with his two brothers

Dad, a dashing young student at Hendrix College Prep

and sister. At the appropriate age, Annie went away to Harding Academy in Searcy, while the boys attended Hendrix College preparatory school in in Conway. Here my dad lived and studied for four years from 1913-1917, making decent grades in Latin, Greek, Mathematics and Business. His school records show that he acquired his share of demerits for "absence from class," being "out at night" or "playing cards." He was showing signs of becoming a free spirit. Then he confirmed it.

On Valentine's Day, 1917, without telling anyone, he went down to the enlistment office in Conway and joined the Navy. Two months later, America officially entered World War I. He soon found himself serving on the battleship USS *Texas*; shoveling coal as they patrolled the U-boat

infested waters of the Atlantic. Perhaps my father's "escape" to the Navy was the best way he could gain the positive broad prospective that guided him in later life. It was his chance and he took it, even though it hurt his father deeply and was resented by his brothers. Regardless, he held firm and remained in the Navy for seven years.

He was 25 years old when he returned home to marry my mother, a pretty young schoolteacher who was blessed with exceptional strength of mind and body. Together they would face debt, the great flood of 1927 and the added hardship of the Great Depression.

Maybe it was because life was so hard and the realities so harsh that he looked for the extraordinary and unusual in all things. It was his quiet acceptance of adversity and

New recruit in the Navy

Newlyweds, 1922

the way he faced it that turned defeat into victory and ordinary events into extraordinary ones. I'm sure he was not the perfect man I thought him to be as a child, but he tried harder than anyone I have ever known.

His first-born son was injured at birth. Then, at age two, he contracted polio. My father took him to St. Louis to be fitted for braces. He was determined that his son would lead as normal a life as possible. He strapped his son's floundering feet to the pedals of a tricycle and later taught him how to ride a horse, an acquired skill that gave him independence and joy all of his life.

His second child was a beautiful brown-haired little girl with bright eyes and a loving spirit that sent her to watch over and help her older brother. When she was four, the dreaded scarlet fever took her in 24 hours. There were no antibiotics in those days.

There was also no electricity in rural areas like ours. It was always up to my father to trudge out into the dark and fix the failing Delco battery or replenish wood in our stoves. On extremely cold nights he warmed a large bath towel before the stove, wrapped me inside its warmth and tucked me into my bed, snug and safe until morning. We were not allowed to get out of bed until after he had built a fire for us.

I watched him squeeze the ashes from the tip of a burned match in the palm of his hand. When he opened it, he showed me that our own family initial of "M" had magically appeared there, and that made us special. I loved it when he crossed his legs and sat me straddled against his bouncing foot, "Ride a little horsey, go to town, take Miss Sissy girl, but don't fall down." In all of those years, he never did let me down.

When I was sick with ear aches, sore throats, measles, and scarlet fever, he managed to rush to the drugstore two miles away and get back home with a my favorite banana split in a paper cup before it melted. It always made me feel better.

I loved sitting beside him in his dusty truck, watching him forge across turn rows, splashing through muddy ditches. He seemed powerful and sure. I felt secure and important in this chosen seat of honor, reveling in my exclusive time with him.

Early one summer morning he rushed into my room, whispering with great urgency for me to hurry before anyone else was awake. Caught up in his excitement, I threw on my clothes and rushed outside to find the saddled horse waiting to take us into the fields to watch the sun rise. With quiet reverence, we stopped to watch the gray dawn change into a thousand brilliant colors and I knew that I had shared one of his favorite miracles. For a lifetime, I would remember this moment when there was no one else in the whole world except the two of us.

Martha Ann at age 4

Dad, Billy and Martha Ann

My mother took great pride in making my dresses for school programs, but just when I was to play in my next piano recital, she came down with undulant fever. I did not know then that it was an infectious disease caused by contaminated milk, but I did know that she would be ill for some time. The next weekend, my father drove me to Little Rock and the M.M. Cohen Company, where we picked out the prettiest blue nylon tulle dress on the rack. It had tiny bows on the puff sleeves, and Mama said it cost far too much money. At age eleven one of the most awkward ages for a young girl to experience, I felt more beautiful than I would ever feel again.

The first day that he began to teach me how to drive his truck, I looked down to shift the gear and ended up in the ditch. He pulled himself out of the leaning vehicle, carefully assessed the situation, and reassured me that this was all part of the learning process in the beginning of a driving career. Without a word, the two of us began the two-mile walk home to get a tractor to retrieve the truck.

My father took an active role in the agricultural community and was quite proud of his 25 years of faithful service in the Production Credit Association of Lonoke County. In 1933 the Federal Credit Act had been passed by congress to provide short term and intermediate term credit loans to farmers because low interest rates were not available at the time with the economic disaster of the Great Depression. As a member of the board, it was my father's responsibility to review the grant loans to deserving hard working farmers. He took great personal interest in the recipients and could offer them the wisdom of his long-time success as a farmer. I knew, that on a certain day of the month, he would without fail make the 18-mile drive to Lonoke. He was also a long-time member of the Plum Bayou Levee Board to oversee procuring the taxes for draining the land and building levees to mitigate the inevitable flooding that resulted from reclaiming the swamp lands. He enjoyed the annual Ginner's Convention at the Peabody Hotel in Memphis where he could stay abreast of the newest agricultural

Keo Man Named Director of Production Credit Association.

W. N. Morris of Keo and W. W. McCrary of Lonoke were elected directors of the Lonoke County Production Credit Association Tuesday.

Secretary-treasurer H. E. Benton reported to stockholders that more than 450 loans, totaling $196,216, were made to farmers in Lonoke, Pulaski and Prairie counties In 1938.

Mr. Morris was among the speakers who addressed 450 persons, including 390 stockholders.

Plum Bayou Tax Affirmed By Board At Pine Bluff

J. R. Alexander of Scott, chairman, of the Plum Bayou Levee Board, presided over an adjourned meeting of the board at the courthouse at Pine Bluff Tuesday at which a two and a half per cent tax on assessed benefits, voted at the first section of the annual meeting at England May 14, was affirmed.

W. N. Morris of Keo, who succeeds the late J. R. England, and Walter H. Estes of Scott, who succeeds his father, Dr. J. H. Estes of Little Rock, who resigned recently, attended their first meeting.

developments and renewed old friendships. When meetings were held in St. Louis, they always took Billy to see his beloved Cardinals play a game.

I can only recall two specific incidents for which I was punished or severely threatened to be. He could whip off his belt in a flash and that was enough. It never had to be applied. At an early age, I put my hands on my hips and defiantly declared I didn't have to do what he had requested. The minute the words left my mouth, I knew that I had made a grave mistake. Another time, I was given permission to go across the road from his cotton gin office with a friend to have lunch at our filling station and diner. A black man named Jessie made the best hamburger in town. I climbed up on one of the stools at the counter, sat my six-year-old self down and ordered. Assuming the role of a character I had recently seen in a Saturday afternoon Western movie, I spoke with grand authority, "Give me a hamburger and make it snappy!" The next day, when the news reached my father, he brought me back into town to apologize. I was utterly embarrassed, ashamed and greatly humbled by the incident. My father would not tolerate arrogance or a lack of respect for anyone.

I can't remember my Dad giving me long lectures or making great demands of me. Instead, he taught me that nothing was impossible with the right amount of determination. He made me feel that I could accomplish anything that I set my mind to. He was a man of few words who went about his tasks, quietly demonstrating most of the right and true things in the way he lived. He showed me courage, strength, confidence, a sense of worth, and initiative—or what he called "gumption." He left me with an enduring belief in God's miracles and a deep admiration for sunrises.

My Mother

MOTHER'S KITCHEN WAS the center of our world. We each had our favorite dish and she used them to comfort, inspire, reassure, and celebrate the milestones in our lives. Some of her greatest culinary triumphs have been added to an "endangered" list by our modern understanding of nutrition. Others have been rendered obsolete by the required preparation time. Her kitchen has become historically significant to a new generation.

Before the passage of The Rural Electrification Act in 1936, our lights were generated by Delco battery. Before the availability of butane gas, we cooked the fruits of our own garden on a wood burning Home Range.

At least once every summer during the early 1940s, a four-door Ford Sedan came forging its way down a dusty road through the flat fields. From our porch, we could see it trailing a brown cloud that marked its progress toward our house and farm headquarters. The driver was a salesman from J.R. Watkins & Company. He was coming to see my mother because she was always good for a couple of bottles of his giant economy-size pure vanilla extract. Like every other salesman in the area, he timed his annual visit to coincide with lunch.

Around the big oak table in the dining room, my mother happily shared with the Watkins man, the same as she did the State Farm Insurance salesman, the Luzier cosmetic lady, the crop-dusting pilot who often landed in the alfalfa field, and the Methodist preacher who came most Sundays after church. With the same generosity she welcomed the World Book Encyclopedia representative, the surgeon from Little Rock who had removed our tonsils, and a Harvard student from Australia who was staying at our house while studying American farming methods. My mother was a tall, slender woman with large hands and great strength. She greeted her guests at the door, holding the bottom edge of her best apron, fanning it like a little girl tugging on the skirt of her best dress. Her hair curled around the classic beauty of her face as she came from the hot kitchen, breathless with excitement. All of the preparations had been made. She removed her apron. Now she was on stage and her finest performance was about to begin.

She smiled with pride as her guests complimented the excellence of her culinary talents. She had an instinctive natural ability, coupled with years of experience. When she was only nine years old, her mother had died, leaving her responsible for preparing the family meals.

On summer mornings, I would be awakened by the delicious aromas drifting from our kitchen. Mother, along with any help she could find on the farm, were busy shelling peas, cutting up fresh corn, canning tomatoes, simmering strawberry jam on the stove, or making crisp sweet pickles from the prolific crop of cucumbers in her garden.

It was a joy to watch my mother's quick, efficient motions and hear her singing as she stirred a batch of cornbread and poured it into the sizzling black skillet to form a golden crust. I loved to listen to the steady rhythm of her hand whisk as she beat egg whites into the fluffy makings of a towering angel food cake.

Summertime was also a feast of vegetables for lunch every day. My father rose at 4:00 a.m., so he was ready for a large meal at noon. Tender young turnip greens were seasoned with pork side and sugar. Plain yellow squash was laced with sweet onions. Corn was cut from the cob and sautéed in a big black skillet. Green tomatoes were fried in corn meal. Green beans were boiled with new potatoes and tiny butter beans were cooked in butter to enrich their natural sweetness. Cornbread and sliced red tomatoes were always there for the finishing touch.

Summer Sundays meant homemade ice cream and a four-mile trip to the icehouse before church. On our back porch, my father chiseled off a portion of the 10-pound frozen block to put inside a burlap bag and crush it with a sledge hammer while my mother poured a mixture of fresh peaches and cream into the metal container that revolved inside the hand-cranked freezer. We each took our shift turning the handle, hearing the grinding crunch of ice and salt as the cream hardened and the process became more difficult. When the mixture expanded and began to spill over the sides, we knew it was time to cover our frozen creation with towels for insulation and let it "ripen" before lunch.

Long before the neat packages of segregated chicken parts in the supermarket, our mother was not afraid to go right out into the backyard, corner a chicken, grab it by the neck, and sling it in a circular motion until the body separated from the head, flew across the yard, and danced frantically as its life ebbed away. Picking it up by the legs, she bore it into the kitchen where she doused its white feathers with a teakettle of boiling water and plucked it with precision. She then lit a crumpled sheet of newspaper and singed it thoroughly to rid the skin of any residual fuzz. When she cut the bird into parts, she always included the prized wishbone, which has mysteriously disappeared from modern poultry packaging. After she dipped the fresh meat into milk, she dusted it with flour and dropped the pieces one by one into the skillet. Never taking her eyes from the frying pan, she held a big fork in readiness for the proper moment to turn each piece until it was just the right shade of brown on both sides and ready to be piled on my grandmother's blue china platter. Sprinkling flour over the crispy parts remaining in the skillet, she waited for the mixture to turn bronze, adding milk and stirring constantly as it thickened to become the best part of all, "milk gravy."

With quick hands she cut up Crisco and flour into tiny pea-sized morsels and poured in buttermilk to stir up her biscuits. She rolled them out with hard, sure strokes and cut them into little circles with the shell of a small Pet milk can. Sometimes on Christmas morning the process was repeated when my brother, Bobby, brought in fresh quail. Mother ignored the modern-day convention of marinating game birds. They went into the skillet just like chicken and were fried fresh, crisp, and tender.

Mother's Boston cream pie consisted of several layers of light yellow cake, separated by creamy custard with chocolate icing on the top. Sometimes when we had "spend-the-night" company, she fried banana fritters for lunch and served them hot right out of the skillet.

When there were dinner parties in our dining room, we were fed early in the kitchen and then packed off to bed, where we lay straining to hear the adult conversation that eventually lulled us to sleep. Sometimes ladies luncheons inspired Bing cherry salads, tomato aspic, and homemade mayonnaise. But no occasion was so grand to us children as the wiener roast in our front yard.

Our friends from town arrived for these gatherings with their entire families. There was no generation segregation. We built a big fire on the hill and set up long tables made of wooden planks and sawhorses covered with tablecloths.

The buns came from the store, but the relish, chili, and cold slaw were from my mother's kitchen. The guests, young or old, were responsible for cooking their own hot dogs on the end of a tree branch or a wire spear fashioned from an elongated coat hanger. We held the spicy meat over the hot fire until it was charred on the outside, pink and warm on the inside.

For dessert, there was always a large chocolate sheet cake. The icing consisted of cocoa, powdered sugar, and a swig of morning coffee with the double purpose of melting the butter and adding a hint of mocha flavor. Sometimes marshmallows and chopped nuts covered the cake that might have a touch of the fresh banana mashed in the batter.

When guests were coming, Mother hurried to make her table a festive one. Her flower arrangements were exquisite creations with a natural spontaneous beauty. They were always done at the last minute, and no two were ever the same. Her centerpieces often contained unusual materials and on occasion, dangerous ones. Once she gathered milkweed along the side of the road. As she admired the lovely white edges of its leaves, an allergic reaction prompted a trip to the doctor and a delayed dinner.

For more traditional materials, she took great pride in the proliferate clumps of daisies that she displayed on the baby grand piano. She adored her pink "surprise" lilies that popped from nowhere every July. On the other hand, she didn't care for the orange day lilies that lined our driveway and didn't mind that we played "house" with them, stripping the petals for "pretend" table fare.

Every summer she grew a whole garden of pink zinnias. After arranging them in her favorite green glass container that once served as her mother's punch bowl, she stood back to enjoy the results of her seemingly careless but effective efforts. Early in the morning when she came in from the garden, holding the moist blossoms in her arms, I could hear her singing an old hymn, "I come to the garden alone while the dew is still on the roses."

The first frost heralded "hog killing" time. Early in the morning when our breath formed a mist in the cold air, the prime hogs were slaughtered. This meant fresh bacon, side meat for cooking greens, hog cheese, chitterlings, smoked ham, and

Billy, Bobby and Sissy

sausage spiced with pepper and sage. In the winter, there were pork roasts and sweet potatoes. When we were at home from school on cold Saturday mornings, we found a big pot of spaghetti sauce already simmering on the stove when we came into the kitchen for breakfast. When we came home from church on Sunday, a standing rib roast was waiting with potatoes oven browned in the meat juices.

On Christmas morning, when we rushed into the living room to gather around the tree, the delicious scent of a roasting turkey filled the house. Mother always rose at 4:00 a.m. on this holiday to assure the bird's readiness before the relatives arrived. She was especially particular about her turkey dressing—it seemed no one else's version could please her. She allowed "light bread" (the store-bought variety) to become stale and almost crisp. She then made a fresh batch of cornbread, crumbled the breads together, and added them to sautéed onions, celery, a couple of eggs, plenty of sage, turkey broth, and enough "sweet" milk (as opposed to butter milk) to give it a near-liquid consistency. The complicated mixture was then placed in the oven to be baked until it was brown on top but never dry inside.

Mother also made eggnog early each Christmas morning. This delicacy was limited to adult consumption because it was heavily endowed with Daddy's secret supply of bourbon. We never noticed our exclusion because Mother's boiled custard with whipped cream was much more to our taste.

When coconut was needed for desserts like cakes and ambrosia, it didn't come from the store. Mother banged an ugly brown coconut shells with a hammer to find the white meat inside. Taking the broken pieces, she carefully cut away its hairy surface and grated the remains into mounds of moist snow. This was used to cover her white cake or stirred into ambrosia along with fresh oranges that were then a seasonal fruit, only obtainable at Christmas time.

Winter was also the time for fruitcakes and jam cakes with caramel icing. Mother claimed that caramel icing was her greatest challenge. She had to be very careful to let the white sugar brown just enough without burning before adding cream to the skillet.

The meringue on her chocolate or lemon cream pies stood tall and firm, and she knew exactly how to add the thickened white sauce slowly into the beaten eggs for the filling in her dessert pastries. Her cream puffs popped up larger than baseballs. Biting down on that crusty bubble would send whiffs of powdered sugar to cover our noses like some magical dust.

There was truly a sense of magic in my mother's kitchen. She instinctively knew "just how long" and how much was "just enough" to come forth with something that was "just right." I have often thought that she had been granted a secret power at age nine to make up for the loss of her own mother. Her vibrant energy probably stemmed in part from the necessity of adapting to the rigorous schedule of her father who was a country doctor practicing in Keo. She told me that immediately after her mother's funeral, he assigned her to prepare his breakfast the next morning. The circumstances of life forced her to be independent at a tender age, but that made her capable for the work that lay ahead.

She spoke very little about those early years in her life but I gleaned bits and pieces from our casual conversations. I always thought that she lived with her father until her marriage, but she had instead moved to the town of England, four miles away to live with some of her mother's family. She always spoke fondly of Idelle Tolsen, who lived next door and would become her confident and faithful friend for a life-time. She graduated from Morris High School, ironically named for my father's family in that area. She received the coveted and necessary certificate to began teaching the next fall in the Tomberlin school system which was seven miles away.

Though, she talked little about those years, she loved to tell the story about falling in love with my father, long before she ever met him in person. It was through the stories that his sister, Annie, would tell her and the letters she shared from the battleship, *Texas*, that intrigued her. When my father returned home from the war, it did not take long for the romance to blossom.

"He came to call on me one warm July night. He took me out on the porch where we sat down in the swing for a moment before he proudly tossed a marriage license into my lap. We were married that very night by a local minister under the tree in his front yard." She always liked to add, " I lacked twenty days of being twenty!"

Her eyes shined with great joy. My, how she loved my Dad and it was returned two-fold for over sixty years. During our talks in the kitchen she once told me, "William Morris has made all of my dreams come true" and he truly did.

I saved all of her clippings, hand written recipes on paper napkins and note cards as well as stacks of recipe books, but I could never quite achieve her proficiency. I searched my memory for bits of culinary wisdom that she shared as she worked but they were all mixed up with her "mother daughter advice" We had our best talks in the kitchen. Years later, I gathered my children in our kitchen to make Christmas cookies or coffee cakes, crack open a coconut or make fudge. The experience always brought us closer together. Maybe that was the magic of Mother's kitchen after all.

Bobby

MY BROTHER BOBBY was two and a half years older than I. He was my best friend. I followed him whenever I could, and I thought he could do just about anything.

Everyone said what a fine looking boy he was. As a matter of fact, they often commented that he looked like a movie star in his senior college picture. I was always proud to be his sister.

Daddy taught him to drive a car when he was nine years old. The principal at our school was so impressed with his mathematical ability that he took his own time to tutor him in algebra in the sixth grade. This set him on an accelerated schedule that sent him to college at 16.

When he was 10 years old, he woke up one day screaming in pain. Having seen the devastation of polio with our brother Billy, Mother and Dad piled us all in the car and drove him straight to Little Rock, hoping some physician there would see us. The

Bobby in our father's arms

test proved that he had rheumatic fever, which meant that he would have to stay in bed for a full year. His bed was placed by a window, where a hole was cut in the screen for him to target practice with a BB gun. He learned to carve wood, make hot pads by weaving wool thread on frames and even embroidered while listening to the radio (long before the days of television).

At the doctor's advice, he went to live with our Aunt Zula in Wyoming for a year. Our world was never quite right without him, but we felt confident that the dry air would be good for him. He came home healthy and happy, with a cowboy hat, cowboy boots, a love for raspberries and a deep bond with his Western cousins, Ross and Gene.

From the earliest times that I can remember, we took piano and voice lessons together. He had perfect pitch and rhythm, and he could play "Boogie Woogie" on the piano. We both won blue ribbons at the Lonoke County Fair one year, but the only lasting significance of all those lessons is that we both sang in church choirs all of our lives.

We tried to play duets together, but he lost patience with my inability to get the right beat and often shoved me off of the piano bench. We did sing a duet once for a Tom Thumb wedding in the big new gymnasium. This time I was angry because he stepped on my dress. I think I kicked him, and he shoved me, but when our names were called to assume our stage roles as members of the wedding party, we walked down the aisle with great restraint, smiling and singing, "As we walk into the sunset into the glow of golden years, I'll always be beside you to dry away your tears." Our common hate for that song reunited us with giggles.

Our disputes never lasted long. Sometimes I had an unfair advantage when Mother took my side, being the only girl and all. My victory was hollow.

I dreamed of going with him frog gigging at night in the bayou, and he finally took me along. It was dark and creepy, and I was miserable, not knowing what was underneath the black water. When his friends began to tease me, he took me home. Later, while I was in college, he allowed me to

Bobby on Little Bits

go duck hunting with him and a crowd of hunters from the surrounding farms. We had only been there a few minutes when I tripped just enough to fill my hip boots with cold water. I shivered silently as we watched the graceful flock of ducks spread their iridescent teal blue wings to land in the water. When the shots shattered the spectacular scene before me, I longed to go home again.

On Friday nights, I rode with my brother in our 1940 Ford Roadster. He took me and my best friend Joy to the movies before he picked up his own date. If the movie was out before he was ready to come home, I was to crawl up in the rumble seat, stay quiet, and pretend I wasn't there, which I was glad to do because he never complained about taking me wherever I needed to go.

I never heard him say a dirty word, and I defended him mightily in the sixth grade when Joy told me she had seen him kiss a girl. One Christmas morning, Bobby and I innocently followed pig tracks down the dirt road, convinced that they were reindeer prints. Later we joined the 4H Club together and tried unsuccessfully to raise chickens and make our fortune. He kept a pet rooster named "Bud" that was bad about digging up Mama's flowers, but Bud would come when Bobby called and that made him a most unique chicken.

Bobby at the University of Arkansas

Bobby once saved a boy from drowning on Clear Lake during a Boy Scout outing. He saved me once when I lost control of my frightened horse. He raced his horse to catch mine, grabbing the reins of my runaway steed and forcing it to turn. He took the time to teach me how to do that for myself right then and there. He taught me a lot of things, like shooting a .22 rifle when he took me quail hunting. The day of his college graduation, he missed celebrating with his friends and drove all night to bring my parents to my Sunday morning baccalaureate service.

With Bobby, it was all about the land and family, and he was faithful to both. He was admitted to Harvard Business School, but after his first year he came back to work on the farm. He worked long hours in the hot sun and long nights in the cotton gin. Until his last days he remembered the details of the old farm methods and equipment, for he was a part of the gradual mechanization. He knew firsthand about the hardships of a working farm and the grueling hours amid the shrilling thunder of a cotton gin screaming into the long nights.

Bobby's Memories

W HEN I ASKED Bobby to help me write this book about our childhood, he met me one day halfway between Little Rock and Memphis. In a roadside restaurant, we found a table away from the crowd and sat down to talk with a tape recorder. Every word was golden to me. We agreed that our childhood had been magical, and he attributed much of that to the place where we lived and the values of our parents and the people around us. I turned on the rather crude recording device and began to record his words, just as he spoke them that afternoon:

In those days, there were no absentee landlords. Farming was all on the sharecrop system. This meant that the tenants worked the land and provided all of the labor. The landowner would provide the seed, fertilizer and whatever was necessary. Once the cotton was picked, the owner would sell it and the profits would be divided 50/50.

As far as cotton-picking wages, a fair estimate would be 200 pounds a day for the average hand. We had a woman at one time who could pick 500, but some could pick only 100. Every member of the family was out picking his own cotton.

If a child were five years old, he would be given a little sack. There were no baby sitters so the mother would take the child to the field.

After the cotton was planted, the weeds had to be chopped with a gooseneck hoe to keep it clean for there were no chemicals. With the little ones their "mama" had to look over her shoulder to help them hoe but they were out there from the time that they were five years old. Of course they had one-row cultivators with a pair of mules that helped a little bit.

In the fall when the crop bolls opened up, there was an onsite, one-bale cotton bed. The tenants would pick all week and fill it up and put it in a covered building until Saturday. It would then be taken on a wagon and hauled to the gin. It was a big day, but the final distribution payment might not be made until the "furnishing" debts were settled.

The first of March, the landlord would give his tenants enough money to live on. They would pay it back on the proceeds of the crop later on, but they were furnished cash every month, enough to buy enough groceries to live on. You had so much to spend and that's all that you got for the month--$15 or $20 a month--it wasn't a whole lot. Of course, in those days no one had a lot of money, and you couldn't carry five dollars of groceries. So that pretty well took care of the season from planting to harvest. My father paid his tenants in cash, not just credit at the store. This was unusual for the time.

One of the first mechanical cotton pickers

Schooling was rather limited because the children picked and chopped the cotton. School was not held during those times. They were all taught to read and write, but that was about it. There were separate black schools, but both the white and black schools had no school buses and no lunches. Teachers were paid thirteen dollars a month. Sometimes they didn't get paid at all. They might be paid with IOU's if the county or the city didn't have enough money in the school budget at the time. Believe it or not, we had small classes and some wonderful teachers at Keo High School. They were some of the best that I ever had, including graduate school at Harvard University.

There was a county health nurse who came around and vaccinated kids for whatever they needed vaccines for. There was a doctor in town that who would treat blacks. People were on the whole pretty healthy. You stayed outside and worked all of the time. You ate good food and didn't have a lot of junk food. There was a University hospital in Little Rock that took care of people without funds. Midwives were on the farm to deliver babies.

The blacksmith was the highest paid man on the farm. He made a dollar and a half a day. That was real high pay. He did not have a crop because the job of sharpening all the plows, welding and maintaining equipment repairs was a full time job. One of the tenants, "Son" McCullough, became the blacksmith after John Taylor died. There were no welders in those days but a good blacksmith could weld the two pieces of iron together by melting them. They had to be good to make it solid. "Son" could do that. I'll never forget his forearms.

There was not as much equipment in the early days, for plowing was done with mules. In the beginning, most labor was done by a mule and a single plow or a mule and cultivator, but you had to be careful to keep the cultivator out of the cotton. In a day's time you would walk at least ten miles. You slept real good at night.

The day began at 4 a.m; that's when the sun came up. That's where the expression "Kin to cant" came from. When it got light enough to see, you went and got your mule and went to work. When the sun went down you put him up. All the farmers knew that expression.

Our first tractor was an Allis-Chalmer tractor with steel lugs. It had a real screwy combination gearshift system on it. There was no hydraulic lift on it, so the two-row cultivator had to be picked up and lowered manually at the end of each row. Needless to say, it took a good man to drive that tractor. The drivers were Aaron Patterson, Cleve Arnold and Henry Harris.

Everybody had a garden and was expected to raise vegetables. They would usually have a hog or a steer to kill for their own beef. The bayou also contained a supply of fish that stayed on the bottom in the hot summers and cold winters. They didn't have to buy any groceries except flour, sugar, salt and pepper. Of course, there were chickens and Guinea hens with the dark meat which was always "good eatin." Turnip greens, squash, okra, corn were in the garden and everyone had onions, turnips and beets.

Kitchens were rather sparse. The pump usually would have been outside the kitchen. There were no refrigerators but iceboxes. An iceman in a truck drove from the ice house in the town of England four miles away. A big block of ice would keep things cool for a while inside the box.

The cooking stove was also used to heat that end of the house. The iron range had an area inside to keep hot water for baths. The stove's wood came from the bayou and had to be cut and split. Hard wood would last longer, much longer.

The mule teams had to be carefully mated. Everyone knew that two certain mules worked together. That's just the way it had to be. Their harnesses were kept separately. The tenants knew the mules and knew when they needed a rest. They all got along great. We first used the horses to herd the cattle; we always had some cattle. Dad had one horse that was strictly his own. It was saddled up for him every morning at daylight so he could make his rounds. It was a gaited horse with a kind of foxtrot or single-foot gait; both better than a trot. There were no quarter horses, just plain horses with names like "Prince," "Beauty" and "Ribbon," who was blind. Ribbon lived to be a ripe old age. Then there was "Little Bits." We got her when I was five and she was two. She died after I went to college when she was over twenty years old. She arrived under the Christmas tree inside the house. She as supposed to be a pet and had never been ridden. When I got on her, she bucked me higher than a kite. She was a smart little horse. She tried to rub me off lots of times against the hedges in the yard.

There was a big flood in 1927. All of the hands came up and stayed in the commissary which, in the early days, supplied groceries and goods on the farm. During the high water, the tenants all lived in the commissary loft. There was an influx of babies that spring, but everybody survived the flood. The water didn't stay up too long, but the watermarks on the cypress siding remained on the houses until they were torn down. A crop was made that year behind the flood. The water came up slowly and left the same way. It just crept up, not at all like a flash flood that you might see on TV. It didn't wash anything away. You just woke up one morning and had water in your front yard. That's when my father had to ride "Ribbon," who "swam" him to Keo to get the mail.

The bayou was full of cypress and tupelo trees. It was originally all cypress but timber cutters took out most of the cypress and tupelo took over. Tupelo was a good furniture wood but still not very marketable. Most of the tenant houses were from tupelo because if you put it up when it was green, it was easy to drive a nail into it. When it dried, you could not pull the nail out so that made it a strong house. The main frame of a house was tupelo but the outside walls were cypress.

Houses are not built like that today, without studs. They would take two-by-fours and make a square and nail it to the frame and that's all it was. All of the buildings lasted fifty years. I never saw one of them fall down.

The bayou had good fishing. It was not stagnant. The water flowed naturally from the cropland into the bayou from one end to the other. In order to reach the other side of the bayou, a dirt dam had been built across it with culverts for water flow. That's where the women sat to fish. They would be lined up from one side to the other. They caught catfish, bream, gar, buffalo and grinnel—a unique variety that have no fins. In recent years, there are fewer fish in the bayou because the chemicals on the crops found their way there. At the other end of the bayou, there was rumored to be a huge snake, so the tenaants would not go there. Water moccasins could be found sun-bathing on tree stumps in the summer. It was fun for me to shoot them with my .22 rifle.

The bayou does not flow today because there is a lift to irrigate from the Arkansas River by way of Plum Bayou. Our father, William Morris, was the first farmer to irrigate cotton. Long ago, his father had planted rice on the farm. At first others said that if you put water on the cotton, it would kill it, but that was not so. He also planted rice again on our farm and other farmers followed.

Our dad was the first to do a lot of things: the first pick-up hay bailer, first two-row cotton picker in the state and the first to use other tools like a "do all" with blades mounted at a precise height, for four rows. Its purpose was to prepare the soil with a flat even surface for seed planting. Our Uncle Gabe

Irrigated cotton field

used the first airplanes for crop dusting and in bad times, was the first to bring in Mexican labor. Both were real innovators. We did something rather unique to pull the irrigation wells. The biggest tractor that we had was 40 horsepower, which wouldn't pull that well. It had a flat pulley on it. If one wouldn't do it, we put two; two belts with one pulley. I've never seen anyone else do that; two tractors, two belts and only one pulley. It really pumped the water from the underground well for irrigation. To dig the irrigation ditches, we had a little "pull-top grader" on a small 30 horse powered tractor. You had to make several passes with lots of shovel loads, just a little at a time.

Even though most of them had no car, the tenants always went to town on Saturday. Our father owned the only two-bale wagons in the country. People would come far and near to see a wagon that would hold two bales of cotton. On Saturdays, John McCullough, who was in charge, often took

Dad in irrigated cotton field

off the sideboards and lined up cane bottom chairs on the bed. Rather than the everyday ropes, John used the leather harness with ornamental red tassels to dress up the mules to take the tenants into town in style.

Walter Bell took care of the horses. He was somewhat of a roust-about. He would saddle up horses for my brother and Dad every morning. He was in charge of mowing the lawn in front of the house and he hated to do it with the hand mower. It was a lot of yard to do with a hand push-type mower but Dad told him that when he got it done, he was through for the day and could go into town. Walter was not much of a tractor driver with two-row equipment. When he came to the end of a row, he would stick out his left hand for a left hand turn in the totally deserted field just as he would in town traffic.

Buster was in charge of the city crew that came to our farm to chop and pick cotton. He wore a jumper or denim jacket with six pockets on it. He would have quarters, dimes, nickels and pennies in their specific pocket. Each worker got their cotton weighed up at the end of a row so they didn't have to lug around so much to the next row. If it were forty pounds, at two cents a pound that was eighty cents, two dollars a hundred. I can still see Buster making change. No one ever questioned Buster. He did the weighing too; that was the important part. The scale was a spring-loaded weight that you could adjust. Some unscrupulous owners might adjust those things short, but not Buster. He was our regular historian. When we asked when we had planted this or that field in soy beans or cotton, he would tell us immediately that we began planting on the 12ᵗʰ of May and ended on the 14ᵗʰ. No one ever questioned that either.

Suddenly, we realized it was time for Bobby to drive back to Little Rock and for me to return to Memphis. Our afternoon together had gone by far too quickly. He had told me so many things I never knew. At the time, I expected we would have many more interviews to discover all that he knew about the farm, but sadly that never happened. I'll always look back upon that day as one of God's many blessings for me to have that time with Bobby, remembering our father, our farm and our young lives together.

Before he left, Bobby handed me a little piece of paper carefully inscribed in pencil in his familiar left-handed writing. It was a list of the indelible and enduring standards and unwritten "laws" that he remembered from our childhood:

1. An optimistic view of life
2. Acceptance of God's will
3. Respect for parents
4. Sharing as a necessity of life
5. Social life centering around the church
6. Required chores
7. Importance of education

When I read that list, I smile, knowing that he lived his whole life faithful to each one.

Keo Methodist Church

IN THE EARLIEST years of the United States, the Methodist clergy travelled around on horseback, covering assigned geographic territories to minister to settlers and organize congregations. These frontier travelling clergy became known unofficially as "Circuit Riders." Our Keo Methodist Church was a descendent of this tradition, as we shared a minister with other towns such as Tomberlin, Humnoke and England, Arkansas. Sometimes the preacher would alternate Sundays or service times to preach in more than one church on the same day.

My grandfather had given the land for the simple white wooden structure which was built on the edge of town in 1907. In the beginning, the Keo Methodist Church had no Sunday school rooms, so classes were held in the sanctuary with portable dividing screens for some degree of privacy. It wasn't until I had moved away that they finally built an addition to house the Sunday school classes.

For a time during my childhood, there was a parsonage next to the sanctuary. I especially remember two ministers who lived in that modest white clapboard house and became not only our pastors, but close personal friends to our family. Brother Dean stood tall in our pulpit and spoke in a deep resonant voice that filled our small sanctuary with his God-given wisdom. He and his wife Thelma had one son who was my brother's age.

During War II, when Brother Dean was called to serve as a chaplain in the U.S. Army, he invited our entire family to come to Brooklyn and spend a week in the generous rambling house provided by the government. The Deans introduced us to pizza and took us to see *Oklahoma!*, our first Broadway show.

Brother Vaught had just graduated from seminary when he arrived in Keo. This young, single preacher immediately stole the heart of one of our prettiest congregational members. Wedding plans included everyone in our church and never has a couple been surrounded by so much well deserved love and attention.

When I was twelve years old, I rode my horse to the parsonage to discuss joining the church with Brother Vaught. Together we studied what this commitment would mean in my life and what serious responsibilities came with it. On the chosen Sunday, I stood before the congregation while he sprinkled my head gently with a rose that had been dipped into a glass of

Keo Methodist Church

water on the communion table. Throughout my life, I have remembered how this small gesture had changed my life.

Mrs. Leake directed the small choir, which my mother attended most Wednesday nights. Mrs. Virginia, a local schoolteacher, played the old favorite hymns on a spinet piano with a jazzy swing that lifted our hearts with joy every Sunday morning. My Aunt Annie played for Sunday School without the least bit of improvisation and substituted whenever needed. My brother Bobby and I were usually in the choir.

The sanctuary was spotless and there was usually a bouquet from someone's yard on the offering table. Every Sunday, Catherine Mosentine stood beside the pulpit to read the attendance report. She would then turn to the wooden board and slip the proper number card in place. A full house was about thirty.

Mama taught the women's Sunday morning class. She worked on her Bible lesson tirelessly each week with the aid of her series of Methodist study books. Once a month, she attended the church's Women's Missionary Society in the living rooms of the members. Along with others in the Society, she often called on the sick and took them food. In addition, she would crochet a pair of booties for every new baby in the congregation. I loved to go with her when she went to call on the newborns.

When Mrs. Virginia had a baby one year, my mother had a shower for her. I've never forgotten the beautiful centerpiece mama created for her table by covering an umbrella with pink and white crepe paper for the very festive occasion. She had a way of making things special.

Some Sundays we had potluck lunches. We all knew exactly whose dish was the best and worst, always choosing part of the worst so no one got their feelings hurt. It was always good to be surrounded by old friends on Sunday mornings.

My mother believed that in order to "stay close to God", we had to be in church every Sunday morning. This strong tie with the church in our youth brought us a sense of belonging and peace, which we always found as adults wherever we lived. Like our parents before us, Billy, Bobby and I attended church every Sunday of our lives.

The Keo Methodist church continues to thrive and celebrated its 100th year in 2007.

Miracles

OUR PARENTS LOOKED for the wonder in all things and expected the exceptional. When they spoke of miracles, they were not speaking of those beyond the divine laws of nature but they recognized those beneficial occurrences as blessings; gifts from God like the old familiar hymn, "Count your blessings, see what God has done"....

In the 1958, Richard Rodgers and Oscar Hammerstein produced a successful Broadway show, *The Flower Drum Song*. One of its most popular songs had clever lyrics with wisdom of the ages:

"A hundred million miracles are happening every day
And those who say they don't agree
Are those who do not hear and see."

My parents recognized the wonders of God in all things and were grateful for each one.

In 1929, our farm was faced with foreclosure, as were so many others in that dark time. My father was seriously ill with pneumonia, yet he was somehow granted the miraculous strength to make a train trip to St. Louis to save the farm from its creditors.

Mother related the time she had stayed with me in a rented room across the street from the hospital in Little Rock. With no motels available, places like this were a common solution to spending the night in an expensive hospital. In the middle of the night, when my fever began to rise, Mother was desperate for an aspirin. When she reached up to the top of the refrigerator in a dark kitchen, her hand magically touched the vital bottle.

Every winter, the muddy two-mile drive to Keo became a challenge. For years the county had promised to lay gravel over the dirt road that stretched between our house and the main gravel road through town. In the summer it was packed hard or became soft dust, but on a rainy winter morning the red clay at the rising hill would turn to glue. Getting stuck meant walking back home for a truck. On these mornings we squealed with delight when our father gunned the motor at just the right moment and successfully mounted the difficult hill.

Our family had a dog named was Jackie. He was a unique mixed-breed Terrier. He was given to us as a puppy by a relative while our mother was in the grocery store and we were waiting in the car. When Mama returned to find that the animal had already bonded irrevocably with us, she chose not to return it immediately to our Aunt Annie Mae, but instead gave him her blessings.

Sissy and Bobby with Jackie

The peach orchard gate once fell on Jackie's leg, forcing him to run on three legs for the rest of his life. Whenever my brother or I practiced the piano, Jackie would appear from nowhere, run toward the familiar footstool nearby, and hit it just right to scoot toward the piano. There he would settle in to listen to our music.

One winter's night, just a few days before Christmas, we were awakened by

Jackie's unusually loud bark woke us all. I heard the excited shouts as my parents found the empty twin bed next to my sleeping brother engulfed in flames. With the superhuman strength that can come to people in such emergencies, they picked up each end of the burning mattress, pulled it together to smother the fire and carried it outside through the front door. Miraculously, there were no injuries and no damage to the room. The headboard of the one twin bed remains scorched to this day.

We never did determine the cause of the fire, but the day before, Mother had piled almost all of our Christmas gifts on that empty bed when she hurried in from her shopping trip from Little Rock. My parents explained that there must have been some sort of spontaneous combustion that destroyed our gifts and toys. Most of them were never replaced, but given what could have happened, it didn't seem to matter anymore. Our gratitude far outweighed the fleeting disappointment.

There was also a fire that destroyed the barn and all the equipment inside but spared our home. Another time, a tornado consumed all in its path, but left our house standing. Then there was the amazing saga of a 2,000-mile trip to New York in a war-time Ford, with gas rationing cards and a 45-mile an hour speed limit. Just getting there and back was miraculous.

Life never seemed monotonous nor boring—nor did my mother and father's marriage. Mother once leaned over to me in the strictest confidence and confessed, "There has never been a time when that back door slammed and I heard your daddy's footsteps that my heart didn't make a little leap! You know I was married to him a year before I realized that I was taller than he was!"

With the faith of children, my parents believed in God's wisdom and the ultimate goodness of mankind. They were never once embittered by the tragedies of their life. With quiet acceptance of adversity, and with strength in facing its consequences, they always managed to find a miracle.

And the greatest miracle of all was my brother Billy.

Billy with our mother

Billy

MY MOTHER REARED back her shoulders to gather more courage and began reciting the often-repeated words of explanation to a curious new acquaintance:

"Billy was injured at birth and had polio at age two, but he is an amazing child."

In my earliest memory of him, my brother was scooting across the floor on his hands and knees, playing with his Christmas toys and laughing with an honest joy that exploded from his soul. That laughter never grew old, stilted or pretentious during his entire lifetime—nor did he. Even as a child, his arms had developed strength far beyond their years because they carried the load normally assigned to other parts of his body. His left leg was shriveled and thin from the polio. Cerebral Palsy made his right leg drawn and taut from the spasms that constantly pulled its muscles. During the day, he walked upright, with the small fragile leg encircled and supported by a metal brace that stretched all the way to his hip. He flung his right leg at each step to achieve an amazing balance. At bedtime he took off his heavy burden and crawled around the house, scampering with the dexterity of a puppy at play.

One Christmas he found a tiny Shetland pony standing under the Christmas tree inside our house After all of these years, I have the original letter from "Santa Claus" that came with this amazing gift.

Dear Billy and Bobby,

I hope you like your pony, His name is "Little Bits" don't you think that is a nice name? You must be kind to him. Don't ever fight over him and feed him well. He likes candy too.

Now be good boys, Good Bye, Santa

From that point forward, horses were a vital part of Billy's life. His legs, bound by the stirrups, flopped against the saddle as Little Bits trotted down the road. Billy held himself firmly locked in the saddle with great expertise.

As he grew, he graduated to a larger Pinto pony that stood still as a statue while he mounted, pulling himself up with his strong arms clinging to his mane.

One fall morning when Billy was six, Mother dressed him in his best white starched shirt and drove him to school in town, just as she did with each of us. Slinging his leg without crutches or help from anyone else, he climbed up the front steps to the big white frame schoolhouse. Long before people talked about "learning disabilities," he was expected to go to

Billy on pinto pony

school and do his best. He and Mother sat in the living room on school nights and went over his lessons time and again. He would scratch his head in frustration and squirm to get down and play, but she persisted.

Mother developed a close relationship with Billy's teachers. To thank them for their extra attention, she baked gifts for them at Christmas time and made exquisite Valentine's cards for them from magazine pictures and lace paper doilies.

Despite her best efforts, school began to drain Billy's happy spirit. There were fights on the playground and he was even knocked down the stairs. He was called "Jug Head" by rowdy boys who ridiculed the features of his head, misshapen by the cruel forceps.

He was an easy target for such schoolyard bullies. His face grimaced uncontrollably when he began to speak, pulling his words with great effort like an old Victrola recording that had wound down. He used his shirtsleeve to wipe a mouth that constantly drooled in spite of the white handkerchief he carried in his pocket with stern instructions from Mama to keep his chin dry.

His educational experience was becoming unbearable. I could hear my parents whispering in the night long after we had been put into bed. Then a solution miraculously presented itself.

Every Friday night, when we went to Little Rock to buy groceries, we had dinner at a restaurant near the Kroger store. It was owned by an Italian family who had boys away at a Catholic boarding school in Searcy, about three hours from our home.

The next weekend, the whole family made the trek to Searcy to scout out the possibilities. Morris School, which happened to have our name by some strange coincidence, became Billy's winter home for the next seven years, all the way through ninth grade.

On alternate Sundays and sometimes more, we ventured to Searcy and ate lunch with Billy and the Catholic Brothers in the refectory. After all of these years, I can still remember the taste of the home baked bread made by the kind priests who wore heavy brown wool robes and black laced high top shoes. When we arrived, Billy was always waiting on a small incline at the front gate with the first view of the incoming cars. He never waved good-bye, turning to hobble away before we left.

This Methodist boy went to mass each day, learned his rosary, was taught self-discipline and gained a greater knowledge of his God. There he received the excellent education that would enrich his entire life.

At first, when he came home in the summers, I was embarrassed to take my friends back to his cluttered room filled with puzzles, comic books and candy wrappers. I soon learned that those who accepted him and listened to what he had to say were rewarded.

After his ninth-grade graduation, he entered Subiaco, another Catholic boarding school in the same area, where he graduated from high school. Reaching beyond anyone's expectations, he completed one year at Arkansas College in Batesville. There his speech teacher took a great deal of time with him and even let him serve as the backstage prompter for her plays. She gave him confidence and the ability to speak more clearly. He carried her picture in his wallet the rest of his life.

The tasks of living on a college campus, however, proved to be too difficult for him. He came back to the farm to begin what he called "making his rounds" on his horse. In the mornings he visited "shut-ins" and kept up with the families on our farm. He read and listened to his radio each afternoon and had one of the first televisions sets in our community.

He sat on the ground in the dust to pitch for a young baseball team in town. As he grew older, he faithfully kept score for their games. He remained a Cardinal fan all of his life and went with our parents to see their games in St. Louis when they attended Production Credit Association meetings there.

He played checkers each day at Hiram Neal's filling station and later learned the game of chess on a visit with cousins in Chicago. Billy played chess by mail with experts from all over the country and rode the Greyhound bus to chess tournaments in Hot Springs, Little Rock and Memphis. He made friends with the bus drivers on the route to Keo. They usually pulled their huge vehicle off of the highway and drove onto the driveway of the cotton gin to make it more convenient for him. He often carried them a sack of pecans from our pecan orchard that he had shelled himself.

Billy enjoyed every facet of the performing arts. Through years of reading and watching television, his amazing memory had stored up factual information and given him a tremendous knowledge of all forms of entertainment. Having long ago memorized the words to most of the Broadway shows that made the local circuit, he sometimes sang along with the performer—much to the amusement and embarrassment of those of us who accompanied him.

Whether sitting in a movie, the theater, symphony hall, or the Grand Ole Opry in Nashville, he turned to the stranger sitting beside him and asked, "How you been doin'?" Most were at a loss at first, but then they would

Billy's graduation from Subiaco

smile in kindness and ask him the same. Others froze in cold indifference. If the latter response hurt his feelings, it never registered on his face. He merely shrugged his shoulders and with his fine self-image totally intact, he turned to the neighbor on the other side and repeated the question.

Billy cried when he heard Eddie Arnold Sing "Ole Shep" on the radio, and he never missed Bishop Fulton Sheen or the Christmas Eve mass from Rome or the Boston Pops' concerts on television. Once, during a reception after a Symphony Pops concert in Memphis, Arthur Fiedler ignored his adoring crowd while he talked with Billy.

As an adult, he was secretary of the Methodist Men's Breakfast Club and a member of the Democratic Election Commission. His name appeared in a Little Rock newspaper beside that of Winthrop Rockefeller when the governor came to visit Keo. He had a dog, a golf cart, and a job during ginning season. When cotton was being picked, the gin had to run all night to keep up with the volume. It was Billy's job to weigh the large trailers filled with cotton as they drove over the scales during the long nights. He never left his post.

When our father had a massive stroke and sat in a wheelchair, just staring into space, it was Billy who pulled his own wheelchair up beside him and comforted him. When his mother grew older and more forgetful, Billy was there to remember the telephone numbers and remind her to turn off the light and the stove.

As Billy grew older, we grew closer together. I would go get him and bring him to Memphis for concerts and theatre shows. He became friends with my friends, and they would be sure to take him to lunch when he was in town.

On his 65th birthday, he "made his rounds" at his retirement home, in a wheelchair with a cluster of shiny balloons dangling behind. He took each of his friends a piece of his birthday cake. He died the next day.

Billy affected everyone he met; they had no choice. He never knew a fake. It was impossible to be one around him.

Mr. Leake's Drug Store

EVERYONE AGREED IT was quite unusual for a town of 200 to have such a grand drugstore. During the 1930s and '40s, Keo, Arkansas was like any other farming community with three stores, two churches, and a post office. But none of them had a drugstore like Mr. Leake's.

A long marble counter gleamed in the light of a great mirror stretching all the way up to an ornate tin ceiling. A pull on one of the many pearl handles rising from the fountain brought forth root beer, Coca-Cola, butterscotch, or thick chocolate syrup. Small square compartments held fresh pecans and whole cherries. The steel counter below opened to great round cartons of vanilla, strawberry and chocolate ice cream. During a time when few had refrigerators, the endless supply of sparkling crushed ice was wondrous. From his giant controls behind the counter, Mr. Leake could make dreams come true. The possibilities were unlimited.

On the opposite wall of the large room there were glass cases framed in oak, which were filled with patent medicines, cosmetics and school supplies. In the middle were four small round tables with polished mahogany tops and twisted iron legs. Mr. Leake meticulously arranged the matching chairs around the tables each morning.

What made this drugstore unique was the daily production of his

Inside Mr. Leake's Drugstore

homemade chili and Leake's Liniment. Both were made in the back, behind the carved mahogany cabinets that separated the public part of the drugstore from the working area. No one was allowed past the wooden swinging doors except Mr. Leake. On cold days, the aroma of tomato and spices seeped from the mysterious back quarters. At times, the odor mingled with the smell of camphor escaping from the big silver vats in the forbidden storeroom where he brewed his famous liniment.

Mr. Leake had a commanding demeanor, standing over six feet tall with wire-rimmed glasses perched firmly on a large nose. Every morning, without fail, long before anyone else rose, he put on his coat and tie and walked the three blocks from his neat white clapboard house to the drugstore. When he arrived, he surveyed the neat rows of aspirin, cough medicines, shampoos, combs and candies in his glass cases, and checked the chairs around his established row of tables. He then walked through the swinging wooden doors to the back counter where prescriptions were filled.

In one of the many tiny drawers underneath his worktable, he once showed me a stack of worn testimonial letters from people all over the United States praising his liniment. There were stories about toothaches vanishing, the pains of arthritis subsiding and the potential ravages of burns disappearing under the protection of its oily balm. He took great pleasure in reading the faded, reassuring testimonials he had received in the mail.

His simple formula probably contained only camphor, baby oil, alcohol and ether, but he believed in its powers. Believing is so much a part of healing, he always said. We children were certain that one day a large pharmaceutical company would buy his liniment or some national chain might market his chili.

Mrs. Leake was as short as her husband was tall. There was an elegance about her summer voile dresses, even though they had long since given up the pretension of having a waist. Her short gray hair with a slight blue cast was curled at the beauty shop in tight waves around her face. She was a member of the Culture Club in a nearby community and took great pride in the fact that she and Mr. Leake had two college-educated daughters and a son who was president of Liggett Myers Tobacco Corporation in New York.

Mrs. Leake commented with great authority on the latest novels and world affairs to the ladies assembled around the tables in the drugstore. Just as St. Mark's Square in Venice was reputed to be the "drawing room of the world," Mr. Leake's drugstore was the living room of our town. It was a gathering place in the mornings after the mail came in and again at 4:30 in the afternoon when the evening newspaper arrived from Little Rock.

Sometimes when there were no waiting customers, Mr. Leake walked from behind the counter, turned one of those small chairs around and straddled it, leaning against the wire back to join the circle and hear the latest news. At times, he made his own contributions, gleaned from early morning conversations with his daughters. Over the wall at the end of the soda fountain hung a hand-cranked telephone box.

When someone came in with a prescription, he quickly assumed a different role, disappearing behind the counter to fill the order in private. He returned through the wooden doors, relaying instructions carefully, repeating them until he was sure they were understood. Many of his customers could not read. He took no less time with the children who came into his store alone, clutching a nickel. As a small hand stretched up to the insurmountable marble counter with a coin, Mr. Leake walked around the barrier and bent down to deliver the requested "cone of cream."

The day before I left to go away to school, Mr. Leake took me aside, looked straight into my eyes and said, "Now, you do your best; study hard. You're going to make us famous someday." I noted that his tall straight shoulders were beginning to stoop. I thought that I detected a little unsteadiness in his walk.

When I boarded the train the next day, the flat, thin bottle with a peach colored label marked "Leake's Liniment" was tucked in my cosmetic case. I felt better knowing it was there. After almost 70 years, I found the old discolored bottle still hidden in my medicine cabinet. Mr. Leake never sold his liniment formula for a fortune or became world famous for his chili recipe. Most of the people who knew him are gone now. His drugstore closed the day he died. The empty building was left dark and deserted for years, but something exciting has happened there.

Two of the local residents opened a restaurant there, and Mr. Leake's drugstore is so crowded at lunchtime that they have opened up the "forbidden" back room for the overflow. They say their older customers

Above is a picture of the very bottle of Leake's liniment that I took away to college over seventy years ago.

Today, there is an enormous mural of his liniment painted on the outside concrete wall of Mr. Leake's old drugstore building.

come back because they remember. Another generation comes because they have heard the stories and found the food to be excellent, especially their famous meringue pies. The beautiful old wooden cabinets are now filled with antiques from the shops that have sprung up in the town. In a place of honor, several empty bottles of Leake's Liniment are displayed along with testimonial letters from satisfied customers.

As a child in those drab Depression days, I thought that Mr. Leake could make anything possible. I still do.

Aaron

IT WAS THE first time anyone could remember the bayou freezing over. During the night the dark water was transformed into white crystal. Ice coated the trees, turning their branches into fragile glass, cracking and shattering as they touched in the wind.

In the winter, Aaron wore his long World War I army coat. With his tall strong body draped in drab green wool, he looked as though he could have been royalty or chief of some ancient tribe. The earflaps of his leather cap hung loosely around his light brown face, distinguished by high cheekbones, the mark of some Indian ancestor. My first Arkansas history book contained a whole chapter on an ancient Indian mound rising from a cotton field in the community of Toltec a few miles down the highway.

Aaron Elijah Patterson was proud of his Biblical name and the fact that his competence had earned him the prestige of being the "main" tractor driver on the farm. He hated winter weather and hovering around the tin stove in the living room of his two-room house, but springtime would soon come. That is when he climbed upon the tractor with its powerful iron lug wheels to lay straight precise rows in preparation for the new seeds and a new crop. But winter was a time for endless waiting, and he was glad when it came time to slip under the warm covers beside his wife, Cora, and go to sleep.

On one of those cold winter days, we children found a new playground on the frozen bayou. Running behind our mother's requisitioned vanity chair until we reached the necessary speed, we jumped onto the seat and sped across the ice for a thrilling ride. My brother Bobby built a wooden sled from rough lumber nailed together with crude runners down both sides. It took us gliding down the hill beside our house all of the way to the edge of the frozen water.

When darkness came, we were called in to supper. Our eyes grew heavy in the warm kitchen and we were soon put to bed. The coal oil lanterns twinkling in the tenant shacks went out one by one. In the still frozen night, sleep came quickly to us all. But it would not last long.

There was a loud knock on our front door. While my father hurriedly slipped on his trousers, the desperate caller shook the single latch on the screen door. There had never been any need for locks. We children hurried on bare feet to see who was there. Oftentimes the tenants were sick and needed to be taken to a doctor, or there was some family squabble that had to be settled. Our father would stand on the back doorsteps, talking quietly to a drunken husband and a sobbing wife before sending them home with new resolutions.

This time, it was the sheriff from town with two deputies. The living room seemed to shake under the weight of their heavy boots as they came inside. I moved closer behind my father when I saw the large guns at their waists.

"Mr. William, we've had a little trouble with one of your tractor drivers out here. He don't much want to cooperate with us. We heard that honkytonk in town is getting whiskey from a still out here in this snake-infested bayou. They say Aaron knows where it is but we can't get nothin' out of him. Thought you might be able to help us. He's out back waiting on the porch."

My father waited a moment and asked, "Has he broken any laws?"

The sheriff shook his head. "Naw, Mr. William, we don't think he has anything to do with it, 'cept he's bound to know where the thing is. We figured if we put him out there on that iced-over bayou, he might tell us, but he's tough and he ain't hurt…just a little cold right now."

My father hurried outside where the moon was shining down on the icy back steps. My brother and I ran through our bedroom and hid on the porch behind the old washing machine where we could see Aaron standing alone. I had never seen him without his leather cap with the flaps, winter or summer. His broad shoulders stooped unnaturally and his eyes looked down as though his spirit had given up. I could barely hear him speak,

"It was so cold standin' out there on that bayou in my bare feets, Mr. William," Aaron said. Everyone on the farm called my father by his first name because they had known him all of his life.

"The pain was a terrible thing. They kept askin' me over and over where that whiskey still was. I don't know, Mr. William, and even if I did, I couldn't tell nobody, cause they'd kill me, for sure."

My father's awkward hand reached toward the familiar coat and touched Aaron's arm in silent apology. Then he spoke firmly, "Go on home and get warm. Tell Cora it's going to be all right. I'll take care of this."

My father turned now in anger and stalked into his bedroom. In the darkness he opened the top drawer of his dresser where his hands felt the cold metal of a silver pistol. He quickly buckled its holster around his waist and returned to the living room. I saw his fingers close around the pearl handle as he spoke.

"You know you made me a deputy, if you remember. I'm supposed to take care of these families and keep peace out here. What you did tonight doesn't help. You know it wasn't right. I've always welcomed you here when anyone needed the law. You know I've been fair, but tonight, you've gone too far. Aaron doesn't know where that still is. Don't ever lay a hand on any of my people again without talking with me first!"

The men left quickly, slamming the screen door. My father stood on the porch until their car lights disappeared down the road winding back to town. Dawn was just beginning to break through the trees as Aaron plodded slowly down the frozen road toward home. His weary body ached but he was safe now. He noticed that the ice was beginning to melt on the edge of the bayou. Spring would come again. His pace quickened with new hope. It was not until much later that one of the greatest tragedies of the bayou occurred.

Aaron named his only child Aaron Elijah Patterson, Jr., but we always called him "Tweet." He was shy and never spoke a whole lot, but we all loved him because Aaron and Cora were so proud of him. Everyone knew that he had a hard time seeing, squinting helplessly when we played in our front yard. It was a great day when my father took him into Little Rock to be fitted for glasses. The years passed and Tweet grew tall as his dad.

One night, ready for his first taste of manhood, Tweet ventured from the bayou to the backside of town and the forbidden honkytonk there. They told us later that one of the rowdy customers was sitting at a table flashing his new pistol. He bragged to the crowd that he would shoot the next man who walked through the door, whoever it happened to be. It was Tweet.

Tea at Roxie's

"THIS IS DELICIOUS tea, Mrs. Green," I announced in an adult tone as my small fingers closed around an imaginary cup and lifted it to my lips. I sat on an old stump facing Roxie, who was holding court under the only shade tree in her front yard.

"And would you have another cookie, Mrs. Jones?" Roxie asked as she passed a large cottonwood leaf precariously supporting three pieces of withered orange peelings. This ritual was often performed on long, hot summer afternoons in Roxie's front yard. It was the time when everyone took an afternoon nap and I sneaked out the back door and over the barbed wire fence to Roxie's house.

People said that the widow Roxie was "all dried up" because her agile body was so thin. Her ebony skin was tightly stretched across her small, sharp features. No strand of her hair was visible under the cotton stocking cap that she pulled over her head and tied in a little knot at the top. The pinch of snuff tucked deep in the trench at the bottom of her lower gum gave her chin an unnatural lump below the lip. There was no way to tell how old she was.

Roxie lived by the pasture fence on a ridge overlooking the bayou. Her house had a porch across the front. No grass grew in the yard. She scraped the ground clean with a hoe to discourage the water moccasins that lived in the murky waters across the dirt road.

She chopped away at the tenacious crabgrass with the same efficiency that she attacked the weeds choking the tender new cotton plants of early summer. She was not the best cotton chopper on the place, but she enjoyed the reputation of being the most prolific cotton picker by far. As her tiny body dragged the long canvas sack strapped over her shoulder down the rows, her quick hands worked unceasingly, pulling the soft cotton wedges from their brittle brown encasement. Her companions talked and visited, timing their picking to coincide with a good conversation, but Roxie passed them without words, driven by a force that gave her body magical strength.

A cotton wagon with a rusty hand scale attached to it stood in the field, so that at the end of each row she could be relieved of the cotton's weight. When Buster, the foreman, weighed Roxie's bounty and recorded it in the worn notebook kept in his shirt pocket, a sly grin of pride relaxed her tight stoic lips.

On these hot summer afternoons when the cotton was growing and we were waiting for the fall harvest, Roxie was never too busy to stop for a tea party with me. Her voice would take on a formal tone as we began the ritual in her front yard around the iron pot where she boiled her clothes. There was little sign of femininity in her posture. Sitting in a cane bottom chair, she spread her bony knees wide apart with her high top men's work shoes planted firmly against the ground.

I watched Roxie chew the orange peel with relish while I pretended to enjoy the hard dry rind my old friend had carefully saved. When it was time to go, I would summon my most polite voice and say, "I enjoyed the tea, Mrs. Green. Thank you so much for having me."

As I climbed the steps mounted over the fence, she always called out, "Come back soon, Mrs. Jones!"

Many years later, I sat with my three-year-old granddaughter under the shade of a magnolia tree. On impulse I picked up one of the crisp green leaves and passed it to her inquiring, "Would you like a cup of tea, Mrs. Jones?" As my fingers caressed the make-believe China, her bright eyes immediately understood and she lifted an invisible cup to her own lips. As we tasted the delicious magic of Roxie's ancient recipe, I felt her presence there.

Miss Echole and the Bag Swing

OUR BAG SWING was known throughout the countryside. It was worth the long walk out to our house. Some Saturday mornings there might be four or five friends from town taking their turns. You didn't have to be invited to try the bag swing. I used to worry when Feller Blevens plunged forth from the tank and the rope tugged mercilessly under his excessive weight, but it never failed to hold him up.

Every spring my father bought a new ¾-inch rope and strung it across the highest limb of an oak tree at the edge of our front yard. He filled a burlap sack with cottonseed and tied it on the other end of the rope with a large knot. He had salvaged an old metal water tank that was about seven feet tall, turned it upside down and leaned a ladder against it so we could scramble to the top.

With one hand on the rope, we straddled the sack of cottonseed and held on for dear life as we swung across the sky with the wind blowing across our faces. It was a wonderful feeling to lean back and look up at the sun dancing through the leaves, then close our eyes and feel the impetus die down to end our turn. At that point we dutifully relinquished the rope to the next in line.

Sometimes when one person was in the middle of their turn, another companion would scurry up the ladder and wait for the proper moment when they would leap onto the swing. It took precision and a great deal of courage. We clung there together giggling and swinging until we slowed to a stop.

Almost everyone I ever knew had swung on our bag swing at least once—except for Miss Echole."

Miss Echole lived in town with her invalid sister, Daisy. Mama and I often paid an afternoon call on to the two old maid schoolteachers when we drove in to get the evening paper at the post office. As we walked into the small, neat house, we could see Miss Daisy in the next room lying there on a hospital bed in her lavender nightgown. Blue veins showed through her pale transparent skin and the white hair piled atop her head was too thin to cover the pale flesh underneath. Even her soft blue eyes were faded and clouded by time. Fearing the wasting body and the bony fingers that she raised to greet Mama, I stood in the doorway and waited while they visited.

Miss Echole, on the other hand, never seemed old. She pulled her gray hair up in a braided circle and wore thick glasses that magnified her eyes and made them seem bigger and brighter. They had a mischievous sparkle and a confidence that spilled over into the way she walked in wide strides like she knew right where she was going. She never owned a car.

One day the principal announced that Miss Daisy had passed away and that school would be dismissed early so that we could attend her funeral that afternoon. I had no way of calling my mother, so I walked to the Methodist Church and stood in line with the other children to view the body of Miss Daisy lying there in her pink satin casket in the front of the sanctuary. I was 10 years old, and it was the first time I had ever known someone who died.

Not long after that, Miss Echole appeared at our door. I was in bed recuperating from a long bout with scarlet fever, but I could hear the surprise in Mama's voice, "Echole Walls, what in the world are you doing here? How did you get all the way out here?"

Mama rushed her in to make her sit down, fearing for her health. Miss Echole turned aside my mother's concern and hurried into my bedroom with her gift. She had spent hours cutting out pictures and words from a magazine to tell a story of my hospital stay, spelling out my name and the story with the pasted letters. I saved it with my most valuable keepsakes. It was quite clever.

As she sat on the side of my bed to talk with me, I saw Miss Echole look out my window to the big oak tree and the bag swing hanging there.

"Now that's something I've always wanted to do—to come out here and try out that swing I've heard so much about!"

My brother politely walked her outside, not knowing what to expect. From my bedroom, I watched the tiny lady climb the ladder up the water tank and reach for the rope that my brother hesitantly handed to her. She pulled at her skirt trying to maintain her dignity while straddling the large gunnysack filled with cottonseed. Finally, she decided her adventure was more important than modesty. She threw her wiry legs around the bag and dived off the tank in a wide swing. The jolt unleashed her circle of braids, sending her long gray hair tumbling down her shoulders to fly with the wind.

Her laughter rang all of the way back inside my bedroom and for that amazing moment, Mrs. Echole was young again.

Uncle Gabe

I REMEMBER UNCLE GABE walking up the path to our house, handing out dollar bills to all of us children and to all the help on the place. His gaunt, ruddy face was crowned with a thin wisp of reddish blond hair, smoothed down by the brown felt hat he now carried in his hand. There was no extra flesh on the bones that protruded through his khaki work clothes. The smell of whiskey filled the air as he passed. His complexion showed signs of overindulgence and his walk was unsteady.

Uncle Gabe had landed his bi-plane in the lespedeza field behind our house. His entrances always had to be dramatic. Everything associated with my uncle by marriage to my mother's older sister, Sadie, was bigger, more expensive, or more dangerous. He seemed to be tempting fate with his daring exploits and the cruel abuse of his thin body. He made a game of taking daily dares with the Lord.

His unlikely pilot on this particular day was his daughter, Docia. Adored by her father and adoring him, she was often his companion on these wild jaunts, flying from his 2,500-acre farm in Chico County, Arkansas.

He owned some of the richest virgin cotton land in the state. He had become a legend in those Depression days. Most people agreed that "everything he touched turned into gold." Uncle Gabe's ingenuity spawned many of the early Arkansas agricultural techniques. America had just fought a great part of World War I by air. Many surplus warplanes were available, and many unemployed pilots were looking for jobs. Uncle Gabe saw the agricultural potential for aircraft. He was one of the first to take to the air for the distribution of fertilizer and poisons to fight the pesky boll weevil.

Any small aircraft and its potential fascinated him. He began to travel from one air circus to another, barnstorming. He joined the 1930s "jet set" of pilot farmers who played games and held treasure hunts from one farm to another, conveniently landing in the many available hayfields throughout the Arkansas countryside.

It was Uncle Gabe who employed some of the first heavy machinery to clear cheap virgin land and level the fields for proper drainage. He trucked in Mexican labor to chop new spring cotton plants and pick the ripe bolls exploding in the fall. At the time, imported labor was not part of a normal farm operation. Uncle Gabe had worked his way up to farm manager for a wealthy landowner. From this unique vantage point he acquired an abundance of cheap virgin land in the backwoods of Arkansas without the encumbrance of sharecroppers. He needed a labor force and he knew where to get it. With his strong interest in aviation, he was one of the first to employ airplanes for crop dusting in the South. For pure pleasure, he often indulged in attending air circuses and watching the antics of local brainstorming.

Once in the summer when we were spending the night on his farm, some of the Mexican workers, wearing broad native hats and carrying guitars, came up to the main house in the evening to serenade us. It all seemed so romantic to me until I learned much later that they had stood up like cattle in big trucks all of the way from Mexico to Arkansas. They may have stayed in abandoned sheds, but mostly I heard that they camped out in the open during their stay on the farm. Regardless of the conditions, they returned every summer.

Aunt Sadie's house began as a modest white frame structure but rooms were added according to the family's prosperity until it stretched forth into spacious comfort. Most conversations took place in the breakfast room attached to the back of the kitchen. Windows enclosed an old screen porch where the bright morning sun bathed a large round table laden with fresh sausage, biscuits and bacon from hogs killed on the place.

Uncle Gabe entertained us by the hour with his tales of shrewd business dealings, gambling escapades, and practical jokes. Aunt Sadie sat beside him, watching and worshiping his movement. When the stream of profanity exploded in front of us children, she mildly protested with a giggle, "Now Gabe!"

Gabe Webb freely adopted lost souls at random. There always seemed to be menagerie of strange individuals in his household. Oftentimes, there was no rhyme or reason for the recipients of his generosity. Once he acquired the adoration of a small red-headed boy with freckled face whom he called Peck. Before the boy was old enough to have a license, Uncle Gabe taught him to drive his car, even though he usually had a driver. His condition was not always conducive to the long distances that he drove when he went on what was referred to as "Gabe's toots." The family might not hear from him for days.

On many Christmas mornings we traveled the long road down to Chico County. A holiday spent at Uncle Gabe's house was a grand affair with plenty for all. I especially remember finding one of the largest Christmas trees that I had ever seen there in the living room.

In order to reach his farm, it was necessary to cross over Mason Lake on a wobbly wooden bridge with no rails. I always closed my eyes to hear the loose planks flapping under the tires of our car as we drove along the narrow crossing, swaying on stilts deeply embedded in the muddy water below. Everything associated with Uncle Gabe was precariously close to the edge. Life was a wonderful celebration, centered on the whims of Gabe and his girls.

Since we lived near Little Rock, Aunt Sadie sent her two daughters to our house to attend the holiday parties in town. There was great flurry and excitement as they unloaded the car with their many suitcases. I watched as they unpacked a shining dress of midnight blue encrusted in rhinestones and a pink crepe sparkling with golden threads woven in its expensive fabric. I remember these specifically, for they were later given to me to play "dress up." I kept them in my doll trunk. Sometimes when my best friend came out to spend the day we stretched a string across one end of the garage and hung a theater curtain made of an old white sheet. Dressed in gowns that would have rivaled those of Ginger Rogers, we danced across the dusty stage that became a grand marble ballroom in our imagination.

Once, the glamorous cousins begged to take me with them and their latest beaus. We drove past town to the highway. Wearing their lovely dresses and reeking of expensive perfume, they stopped their shiny Ford Roadster in the middle of the highway. Leaving the headlights to burn and the car radio to play, they took turns dancing in the middle of the highway. There was really not much chance of a car coming down the lonely road, but the possibility added to the excitement of that night.

On one of his trips to our house, Uncle Gabe coaxed my mother out to the pasture to see his plane. He convinced her to climb inside the cockpit to see what it was like. While she was lost in the wonder of it all, he cranked up the motor and took off. Uncle Gabe dipped and turned that plane, laughing as Mother clung to the seat screaming. She was furious when they finally landed. She later told my father, "With three children, I have no business taking chances like that! My heart was in my mouth. Lord, I yearned for the solid earth and its safety!" That is where our family felt most comfortable riding out the difficult economic days on the farm.

In those early drab years of the Depression, a visit to Uncle Gabe's house made my parents' load seem a little lighter. On the drive home, my father was filled with fresh new ideas, dreams and courage to take the chance to make them come true.

Docia in college

My Cousin Docia

I THOUGHT UNCLE GABE'S daughter Docia was more glamorous than any movie star I had ever seen. When they landed their open biplane in the lespedeza field behind our house, we ran out to greet them. I remember how beautiful and slim she was in her white gabardine jodhpurs with a matching aviator cap snugly snapped under her pretty chin.

Docia was right there when it all began. She shared her father's adventuresome joy in flying and was one of the pioneers who navigated the first small open-air planes. She was the first woman pilot in Arkansas to solo. She flew with Charles Lindbergh and with Jimmy Doolittle. Her exploits had once been chronicled in a front page story of the *Arkansas Democrat*.

I had begged her for years to write down her flying experiences during the 1930s. One day, the mail brought a box of tapes with her strong and sure 87-year-old voice telling her story. I was thrilled to be the one who would get to hear the whole story and preserve it for future generations.

As I began to transcribe her words on paper, I was struck by the primitive conditions of her childhood on the farm and the tremendous responsibilities given her at an early age. She was taught to drive at age seven to help her father load the hay on their first Ford truck. At age nine, she chauffeured her cousins to school over a railway bridge. The legendary and destructive 1927 flood had knocked out all the other routes. Since her car could not straddle the tracks, she forged across each day with one tire on the inside of the track and the other on the outside. It was not that much of a stretch for her to begin flying lessons when she was 22.

As she recorded her aeronautical escapades, the tone of her voice soared with the wonder and excitement of a child:

> This story of my love of flying began on May 21, 1927 when Charles Lindbergh (at age 25) made his transcontinental flight from New York to Paris in the famous *Spirit of St. Louis*. I was 14. We kept our ears glued to a radio to see if he could make such a trip. Well, when there was news of his landing in France, we were thrilled and thankful that God had allowed him the privilege of the success. Then there was the radio news of his arriving back in the U.S. The parades and celebrations for Lindbergh were really something to hear on the radio. His prize was $25,000.

> You can imagine what a great pleasure it was for me to see him in person in 1929 when he landed *The Spirit of St. Louis* in a field right outside our town. He was handsome, cute, kind, and funny. I didn't expect to see him in person again but as luck would have it I had another opportunity in 1932, the year I finished high school. My big break came to me again when Lindbergh came back to our little town barnstorming, but not in his famous plane. (Barnstorming is when a person or a group of persons sell rides and put on air shows.) This time we took an air ride with Charles Lindbergh. What a thrill!

After his famous flight, Lindbergh was engaged by the trustee of the Guggenheim Fund for Promotion of Aeronautics to visit every state in the union. He flew the *Spirit of St. Louis* 22,350 miles, covering the 48 states. He made 147 speeches and Docia was there when he spoke in Little Rock.

In 1935, my Uncle Gabe brought an instructor to the farm to teach Docia to fly. When she seemed to be ready to solo, they proceeded to the Little Rock airport. She remembers that day well:

> After two days of lessons, take offs, and landings, my instructor thought I was ready to do it alone. So sometime about four or five o'clock, I took off. He did not say for me to come right back. So I went for a ride over North Little Rock. I was enjoying my life in the heavens on my own so much that I did not hurry back. When I did decide to return for my landing, all of the floodlights were on at the airport, an ambulance was there, and everyone was standing in front of the hanger waiting for my landing. Well, thank God I came down and made a three-point landing. I was ready to take off again right then, but my instructor said, 'No, we'll start again tomorrow!'

The next time Docia came for lessons in Little Rock, she met Jimmie Doolittle. His achievements during that golden age of aviation were by now legend. He was the first to fly across the US in a single day. He had established a world speed record and made his greatest contribution in the development of instruments for flying in adverse weather. By the time Docia met him, he was manager of Shell Oil Company's Aviation Department.

> He and a couple more pilots, (whose names I can't remember, but I think all of them were later ace flyers in WWII) were

going to fly over to Hot Springs, Arkansas and they invited me to come with them. They said, 'Come and go with us and we shall see if you can fly some on the way over and back.' They did let me pilot—plus they showed me some tricks of the trade, which I appreciated. Of course, I never dreamed they would end up in the war as noted fliers, especially, Jimmie Doolittle!

There was a unique camaraderie among those early pilots. Docia recalled that four army planes once got lost on their way to an air show. Spying some of her father's planes parked below, they landed in the family's field. Her father invited them in for a country lunch of fried chicken, gave them directions and sent them on their way. Another pilot friend gave her the lifetime experience of flying in the very first Stinson, a 4-seated, single-wing plane with an enclosed cabin.

Docia described her near-disaster taking off in a downwind, and how she had to follow the railroad tracks back home when she got lost. She discovered that it took four hours to fly to Memphis in a headwind and only one hour to get back with a tailwind. Most of her lessons came from first hand experience. She laments, "But me, I never did get my license to fly. I did have enough hours too, but my future husband came along in 1937 and we became a pair for life."

Her deep interest in planes and flying, however, never ended. During the 1950s, she had a private tour of Langley Field in Virginia and was fascinated by how "they taught our men to fly." While attending an old-fashioned barnstorming and antique show in San Bernadino, California, she found a Waco biplane, though "it was not a Waco J-10 like we used on the farm for pleasure flying and dusting cotton." She went to Long Beach in 1983 to see Howard Hughes' famous *Spruce Goose*.

It was the largest airplane I have ever had the opportunity
to see. There were so many things on the instrument board
to learn and know about. I could stand up straight to walk
under the wings and the belly of the plane was a huge room.
I would never dream it could be so large.

Despite all her ground-breaking accomplishments, she sounded proudest
when she told me about her son being a gunner on a helicopter in Vietnam.
When he returned to California, he trained to become a pilot but did not
tell his mother. He called and said he wanted to take her and his father to
Catalina Island. He took them to an airplane he had rented and announced
that he was going to be their pilot!

Oh me, what a big thrill to have him fly us over the island and
land at the airport! We were so pleased and thankful that God
had been with him in the war and now allowed him to do
what he wanted to do very, very much – fly an airplane!

She ended her narration on the happy note of her son's triumph. She
began with the words that seem to summarize her life:

There have been many hardships and many disappointments,
but much joy in the happy times. To see so many different
stages of life, the growth and changes in this world has been
a wonder beyond any dream I could dream.

She never lost her wonderful enthusiasm and optimism. In her last years,
Docia divided her time between her two sons in California and Chicago, so
she continued to soar frequently on commercial airlines. I think her wisdom
and deep gratitude for all of life came from her elevated perspective as a

pilot. From her sky view, all of the small and insignificant things lost their importance. She said of her first solo flight, "I was enjoying my life in heavens on my own so much that I did not hurry back!

I, too, was reluctant to leave the magic of her world.

Helena and Poochie

HELENA AND POOCHIE were the children of our cook, Mable May. Most summer mornings we found them waiting for us under the oak tree in the front yard. Sometimes we would all pile on the bag swing, clinging to each other. We could not foresee the turmoil that would come some 20 years and 20 miles away in Little Rock, when hate at Central High School would change the entire world.

Their mother walked up to our house every morning after breakfast and picked fresh vegetables from our garden and cooked them in black pots on our kitchen range. She was determined for her children to attend classes in the tiny schoolhouse on the back side of town and was strict in her teachings about being clean, working hard, "trying to be somebody" and "knowing your place." She spoke often about "good peoples" and bad ones, and spared no words in lecturing us on respecting our elders, black as well as white. She insisted that Helena and Poochie finish their chores before they came up to our house.

"Poochie's almost a man now. He's so growed up but then he ain't nothin' but a chile and has to play sometimes." Poochie was near my brother's age, going on 12, but he was already acquiring the powerful shoulders and arms of a man. When a smile broke across his dark round face he was the image of Mabel May. He was good-natured and nothing seemed to bothered him. Helena, pronounced "Heleeeena," was a little younger than I was. Her thin legs seemed too long under the short cotton dress she had outgrown. She had a pretty, fragile face and light brown skin with black coarse braids across the top of her head.

We followed our older brothers around, perfectly willing to endure the indignities imposed on little sisters in order to be allowed to accompany them on their fishing expedition down at the bayou. It was the shaded waters of the bayou that broke the hopeless monotony of summer and for a child— it was magic. Almost every morning during the summer months we headed for the bayou, often with Poochie and Helena. We captured tadpoles in fruit jars and looked for the miracle of baby frogs. With a cane pole we caught a wide variety of swimming things including a strange 4-legged reptile-like creature called a lamprey eel.

We kept a homemade wooden boat at the clearing near our house. With a hand chiseled paddle we pushed off from a muddy bank into the water and navigated through thick brush into the sanctuary in the middle of the bayou. Sometimes my brother Bobby and I sat there quietly, hypnotized by the frightening beauty of the cool green place.

One day we ran barefooted along the soft, dusty road trying to keep up with our brothers' pace until they approached the edge of the water where the homemade wooden boat was tied. We followed them to down to the bank where we sensed the dank smell of fish and stagnant water. As our feet began to sink into the mud, we stepped back to the safety of the grass and watched.

Finding the familiar craft half full of black water, the boys retrieved a tin can that remained in the boat as standard equipment and began dipping until they had removed enough liquid to stay afloat. They shoved off in the makeshift craft leaving us behind on the bank.

Poochie stood in the front, guiding the boat through the shallow water with a wooden paddle that dug into the soft muddy bottom to serve as leverage. As the water grew deeper, the heavy paddle slipped from his hands and he helplessly watched the boat glide past. He instinctively lunged out to retrieve his lost steering apparatus. Instead, he plunged right into the deep forbidden water, head first.

There was a great thrashing as Poochie struggled to free himself from the suction that held his head and hands trapped in the soft mud. All we could see were his feet kicking wildly in the water. Helena and I laughed at this ridiculous sight until we thought about the water moccasins that often slid through the water. I watched my brother reach for tree branches above him in an effort to push the boat toward Poochie. As soon as he was near enough, he grabbed Poochie's feet and pulled. When Poochie's head rose above the water, it was covered with oozing mud and he was gasping for breath. His frightened eyes searched for something to hold on to as his hands slapped the water desperately. My brother leaned over to grasp Poochie's hand and drag him toward the boat, which was leaning precariously near dipping into the water. Poochie clung to the side until he had gained enough strength to pull himself back into the cumbersome vessel.

He sat upright trembling silently as his eyes stared into some far away place. The mud on his face and hair began to dry in the summer sun. My brother shoved against the nearest tree and used his bare hand to paddle back to shore. I heard Helena shout with nervous relief, "Mama's goin' kill you for messin' up your clothes like that!"

Poochie didn't answer. With the mechanical reflex of a robot, he reached down and helped Bobby pull the boat up on the bank. He turned to walk toward his home without a word to any of us. What he had seen and imagined down there in that black water was more than he could take in, more than the rest of us could ever understand. Everything was different now.

Our School House and
the Shining New Gymnasium

EVERY MORNING DURING the school year, a bell tolled from the steeple rising over the school in Keo which I attended from the first grade through the fifth.

The schoolhouse was a rambling old frame building with a flaking whitewashed exterior. Inside the black wooden floors carried the strong scent of fresh oil that had been applied to absorb the coal dust filtering from the iron stoves in the center of each classroom. There was no indoor plumbing. My father had begun his education in the same old building.

Because there were no school buses, many students walked a good distance from their farm homes to attend class. Once we arrived, we were taught by an excellent faculty of strict yet devoted teachers. We were to learn the "three Rs" and despite the Spartan facility, we did just that.

At recess, we chose sides among our friends without the necessity of any adult supervision. We played baseball, jumped our ropes, drew circles in the dirt for a game of marbles or made squares for hopscotch. Playground equipment was unheard of. Sometimes collecting Hygrade coupons from school tablets generated a new basketball for a game of "keep away."

The largest room in the schoolhouse was the auditorium. Wooden

Keo School House, Grades 1-12

seats, darkened by the passage of time, were bolted to the wooden floor in immovable rows. The stage was hidden behind a painted canvas curtain that rolled up and down on a heavy spindle operated by a maze of ropes hanging in the wings. Across its expanse were printed the names of various businesses in the community that had contributed to this portion of our educational development.

This dark hall that housed our Friday morning assemblies became a showcase for our local talent in the evenings. Our school auditorium was the Lincoln Center, the opera house and Broadway for this town of 200. There was a yearly senior play, voice and piano recitals, and variety acts in the framework of minstrels or Tom Thumb weddings. Here one could enjoy a rendition of Jeanette MacDonald's "Sweetheart" or "Indian Love Call," John Thompson's "From a Wigwam" or a Chopin Etude. Once, I remember a young artist sat at an easel on stage drawing pencil caricatures of local citizens. If you had a glimmer of talent, you would appear on that stage sooner or later.

In addition to our school studies, my brother and I took piano and voice lessons twice a week for 50 cents each and practiced an hour each day. Our voice teacher, Mrs. Roper, had a blond braid encircling her youthful white Dresden face. Our piano teacher lived in an elegant Spanish-style home near the school, reminiscent of her once affluent life. Her bony, arthritic fingers bloomed out grotesquely large at the end. Her jet-black dyed hair was too thin to cover her head completely. She wore silver pince-nez glasses pinned on one of her two timeworn knit dresses. They were "spring-loaded" so she could pull them in and out to read the music I was playing.

Preparation for a performance took dedication, but we considered it to be a joyful endeavor. We were driven by the anticipation of a live performance on stage when the footlights would burn our faces and the enthusiastic applause would fire our souls. One year, my brother and I won two blue ribbons in the voice division at the Lonoke County Music Fair. I had a fever of 103 when I performed, but then, that was show business!

The school's only athletic program centered around the two basketball goals on the back of our dusty schoolyard. The game was a natural choice for our high school students because a team only required five players, and we never had many more than that in a whole graduating class.

The dirt on the homemade outdoor "court" was worn hard and smooth. Training there produced a fairly good basketball team that played other outdoor groups from the surrounding small towns. Unfortunately, bad weather often robbed them of the practice time necessary to compete with schools that had a real gymnasium.

Then one day, when I was seven years old, government officials arrived and began to survey the playground and the empty lot next door. Word spread and rumors flew about our potential new educational facility. Soon the official announcement was made: the school at Keo was getting a brand new gym.

It was an exciting time for us as we watched the construction each day. First the concrete foundation was laid. Then the walls rose to a giant vaulted ceiling. A grand, contemporary gymnasium began to unfold next to the old barn-like schoolhouse. Knowing that the entire senior graduating class had never numbered over ten, it would seem an impossible task to assemble a basketball team that would justify a building of such magnificent proportions.

The fine new structure was covered in the most modern white Masonite siding. The shining new basketball court seemed to stretch for acres and acres. We could only venture forth on its glass-like surface in our stocking feet, for none of us owned tennis shoes. We were warned that our own rubber soles would leave ugly black marks on its shining surface. On each side, permanent wooden bleachers rose to the sky. At each corner there was one of four indoor restrooms with plumbing—a luxury we had never enjoyed inside the schoolhouse.

Across the front of this imposing structure was a real concrete sidewalk, only the second one in town. It made possible my first experience on roller skates and a bicycle. We had never before had a hard surface on which to participate in these modern activities. We ate lunch and played jacks on the smooth concrete porches covering the double entrances, but the big gym doors stayed locked except on very special occasions.

This splendid edifice that overshadowed everything else in the town was the work of the WPA (Works Progress Administration), Franklin Delano Roosevelt's answer to the Depression. Rather than giving direct relief to the unemployed, the government provided them with jobs involving everything from digging ditches to writing travel guides. The WPA was often jokingly subtitled "We Piddle Around" to denote the caliber of labor employed in these projects, but the work in our gymnasium proved to be unquestionably superior. Roosevelt had saved the farmers with the first government subsidies, and in 1939 he provided us with the finest sports facility in the state.

Keo School House. Painting by Mary Morris Cardwell.

We took great pride in our new WPA gymnasium. Hazel Walker, a renowned star in Arkansas women's basketball, brought her team down from Little Rock to dedicate the new court in style. There were exhibition matches between the famous Globetrotters and their rivals, the Washington Senators. Our town had become the basketball capitol of the area. It did not seem to matter that we still had a dilapidated schoolhouse.

The first school teams to play in our new gym were coached and sternly counseled by our school principal, Peck Ashcraft. He volunteered even though he already had an overextended schedule teaching Math. I doubt he ever received any additional salary, but the students would never forget the influence he had on their lives. One of the history teachers helped the girls' team. Neither team won any great championship, nor did a scout scoop up any of the players to be professional stars, but what a joy and appreciated privilege it was for them to play on that magnificent court!

Sadly, the gymnasium began to lose its splendor as early as 1950. The war had depleted the population to the point that the school could no longer field a team. The school at Keo became part of the state's first consolidated school system. The gymnasium bleachers were removed and the space converted to classrooms for the children brought in by big yellow buses. Eventually the dwindling number of school-aged residents were bused to a larger town nearby. Both school and gym were torn down. Houses were later built in their place, covering every trace of their existence.

Today the only remnant remaining of the school or the gymnasium is a brass plaque near a small gazebo in the center of town. Some of the alumni put it up as a memorial to their old principal, teacher and basketball coach, Peck Ashcraft.

It would all seem like a dream if it were not for our annual reunions. We met in the Baptist church building next to the former school property and former students came from throughout the United States. We reminisced about our former teachers, the time the maypole got cut down and the glorious days when crowds descended upon our town to bask in the bright lights of our fine gymnasium.

The magnificant gymnasium

Mother's Hats

THERE WAS A large chest in Mother's bedroom. Its long, deep drawers were filled from top to bottom with her hats. The treasure trove included small lacy hats with fragile pastel flowers and dark felts turned in sophisticated shapes, but the ones I liked best were the great round straw circles that seemed as big as an umbrella. The exquisite pattern of the fine woven brim shrouded my mother's face in elegant mystery and seemed appropriately proportioned to her height.

Each hat had a story. When we returned from a shopping trip to Little Rock, she would carry the large box into the living room to greet my father, ripping open the top as she talked. "William, I found this hat today and it was such a perfect color. It was rather expensive, but it is made so beautifully and everyone seemed to think it looked wonderful on me. Do you think it cost too much?"

I could see my father smile as he gazed at her excited face crowned by her latest purchase. "Well, if you like it, Mary, just keep it and quit worrying about the cost!"

I was always exhausted from these shopping expeditions, but Mother would scurry into the kitchen and begin fixing dinner, humming a little tune as she thought of her grand new acquisition.

It was usually in the summer, when I was not in school, that I accompanied my mother on these trips. It always seemed much hotter on Main Street in Little Rock than it did out on the farm. We would walk the length of the street, from one department store to another—Cohens, Pheifer, Blass. She knew each sales lady by name, how many children she had, and who her husband was or when he had died. Most of them were widows who looked forward to mother's visits. She listened to all of their problems and offered her frank opinion and advice. With great patience, they brought out every hat they had that was a shade of beige or brown. My mother had nothing in her wardrobe that was not somewhere in the brown tone. The smartly dressed sales lady would usually say, "I thought it looked like you."

They would discuss the price as though it were impossible, then would search out all of the cheaper varieties before finally returning to the first one with the assurance that Mother "would never be pleased with the inferior quality of the others after having seen the best!"

When I complained about being hungry, Mother would take me to the lunch counter—every department store had one. We would order a toasted sandwich, iced tea in the tall ice cream soda glasses, and a caramel ice cream sundae for dessert. Staring across the counter, preoccupied with her thoughts, she would suddenly turn her stool to face me and ask, "Do you like the hat or do you think I'm foolish to buy it?"

We walked and shopped most of the day. It was always after four o'clock by the time we were through, and the traffic in town slowed our departure. We edged our way to North Little Rock where we parked in front of the Kroger store. Some distant cousin worked behind the meat counter there and saved the best cuts for us. He and Mother had to discuss his entire family and latest crisis before we could go through the checkout counter and start the 25-mile drive home.

Once, as she was sewing late in the afternoon, she stopped the steady rhythm of her foot pumping the pedal of her Singer sewing machine.

Looking out the window, she mused, "You know, I get so lonesome about this time so far out in the country. When I lived in town growing up, we used to visit with each other across the fence about five o'clock. If it weren't for your Daddy, I would miss that."

I thought about the long shopping expeditions and wondered how important the seldom worn hats, carefully tucked in her drawer, really were.

Revival

THERE WAS THE revival of Greek culture in the Roman period. There was the revival of the Roman culture in the Elizabethan period. And every summer in our little town there was another sort of revival—church revivals at both the Methodist and Baptist churches.

The idea was to rekindle the original fervor and emotion of one's religion. For some reason, churches felt called upon to do this when the weather was at its hottest. Often there were tent meetings in the larger towns, but in Keo the yearly revivals were held with dignity inside the church—where it was even hotter.

The unbearable heat was stifling even though the windows were all open. Outside the air was dead still with no breeze. Each pew was supplied with paper hand fans provided by the local funeral home. Everyone fanned shamelessly in an effort to find some comfort in this heat.

On those evenings, at my friend's church, following the preacher's most dramatic sermon, the congregation sang endless verses of, "Just as I Am." While the music continued, those convicted by the minister's words walked with great regret and repentance to the front of the sanctuary, where they pledged to renew their life. On these occasions I usually sat on the front row with my friend. Each year I would see her body become rigid as she rose to walk to the pulpit and join the church all over again. I sat very still and stationary because my mother told me that if I continued to walk with the Lord, joining the church once was enough.

Although we were Methodist, my father attended the Baptist revival at least once during their week. It was a courtesy for the minister to call on one of the distinguished visitors to pray. So one night, he turned with great ceremony to my father and said, "Brother Morris, would you give our closing prayer this evening?"

Everyone bowed their head and waited in anticipation for a humble offering to God. Instead there was an interminable silence. A shuffle arose throughout the crowd as some lowered heads turned awkwardly to determine the location of "Brother Morris."

My father was a wise man. People came to him for advice. He was president of the Production Credit Association, served on the Plum Bayou Levy Board and the Cotton Council, and was a member of the governing body in our Methodist Church. On a one-to-one basis, he knew how to say just the right thing, but in front of an audience, he froze.

In addition, he considered his relationship with his Lord to be a very personal one. So, partially from fear and partially from his stubborn determination not to share his thoughts with the world, he remained silent. The minister was faced with the embarrassing contingency of calling on someone else.

Suddenly, from the other side of the room, a forceful and sure voice broke the painful silence. It was my brother Bobby, who graciously lifted the burden of our father's cross and bore it magnificently.

Since this was now a family endeavor, it seemed to make everything all right. As his son prayed with the fearless eloquence of youth and a year at the University of Arkansas, my father quietly offered thanks to his Lord for his miraculous reprieve.

The Walk Home

THEY SAY THAT I was only three years old at the time. I can no longer separate the often-told details from my own memory, but I can still feel the tears burning on my face in the blistering noon sun as I walked through the hot dust. The softness of the country road was a relief from the sharp gravel rocks in town. I looked back to see how far I had come and hurried my small barefoot steps toward home.

No one had seen me leave town. I had slipped down the driveway as Carrie's maid, Mabel, washed the dishes and put away the lunch things. This time of year most everyone in this small farming community enjoyed a large noon meal followed by a nap in the heat of the day. The town was deserted and so was the road that stretched through the endless cotton fields toward home. The intense heat sent waves and ripples across the straight rows, causing the landscape to move like liquid in the July sun.

I was supposed to be spending the afternoon in town with Carrie, who was a year older than me. She lived across the highway to Little Rock in the only brick house in town. It had ceiling fans that whirled around, stirring a cool breeze through the dark paneled rooms in the summertime.

That day, my mother was having a rare bridge party at our house out on the farm. There had been days of preparation, with the strange smelling chicken salad, the expensive can of Bing cherries and the terrible grown-up tomato Jell-O that Mama called "aspic." It was nothing like anything we usually had around the big oak table with the family. When we had company over to spend the night, she made our favorite things like banana fritters and cream puffs. Today everything had to be just right for the ladies who were coming. The white ruffled organdy curtains had been washed, starched and ironed. The big round green bowl on the piano was filled with pink zinnias from her garden.

Mama always got nervous and in a hurry when she was having company. She was out of breath when she answered my questions absentmindedly this morning. I wondered if she even heard what I was saying.

Since Carrie's mother was invited to the party, I was asked to spend the day in town with her. Carrie had a winter coat with a fur collar, a pony named "Blackie," and a playhouse. She was plagued with mysterious allergies that forced her to live part of the winter in Arizona. When she came home her skin was golden brown from the sun, and she had a funny accent that would change back before we started to school. Some mornings, on the way to school, her mother stopped at the local filling station and short order counter to get her a hamburger. My mother told me that she was an "only child," as though it was an illness of some kind. It made me feel sorry for her.

Everything seemed fine in the beginning. Mabel was busy with her chores around the big house, but she would peek in on us every now and then. It was too hot to go outside, so we first tried a game of Old Maid cards. Then we escaped to the upstairs bedroom closet, which was filled with long-abandoned clothes that Carrie's mother had delegated for playing "dress up." There were filmy dresses of silk georgette, shoes with rhinestones and boxes of hats covered in feathers and beads. When I pulled one of those magical frocks over my braided hair and freckled face, I immediately became a beautiful movie star. But because Carrie was slightly older, it was always she who got to marry Dick Foran, our Saturday afternoon Western movie idol.

That afternoon, when we were tired of the games, we ventured outside with our jump ropes. Mine had bright red handles and bells that jingled when I skipped on the concrete leading to her garage. Carrie's brand new model was made of thick green rubber that lashed the driveway with a frightening force. Suddenly she leaped upon the porch and began flinging the elastic rope in circles, pretending to be a cowgirl lassoing the imaginary "bad guys." Unintentionally, the new weapon struck, and I felt a sting against my bare legs. A sudden anger clicked inside me. I threw down my jump rope and ran right out of her yard in the direction of home.

I hurried across the forbidden concrete highway, sobbing shamelessly as I ran. Luckily, there was very little traffic in those days. I managed to stop crying long enough to make my way unnoticed down the narrow dirt path past the row of modest houses that ended right next to the Methodist church. My anger and determination forced me to a final commitment down the deserted country road.

My only thought was to get home. Home was a safe place along the cool green bayou. I didn't care how long it took. I was going home. As I turned by the pecan orchard, I saw a black man walking toward me. I recognized him because he lived close to me out on the farm. He was dressed in his town clothes, his Sunday dark blue suit and brown polished shoes coated with road dust. Fearing that he would stop me, I looked down at my feet as we passed going in opposite directions.

He inquired politely, "Miss Sissy, what yo' doin' out here on this road this time of day?"

I walked faster, not looking back, but I knew he had turned to follow me home, keeping a safe distance.

I felt my face getting redder in the heat. I was never allowed in the sun without that hated flowered sunbonnet. I passed the Fletcher place. There was no one in the yard; just a few chickens pecking around. A dog barked in the distance. I could see the road rising to the hill where Morris Chapel stood and our land began. The red clay buckshot was dry and dusty now.

The big double doors on the whitewashed wooden chapel were locked. No one was ever around except on Sunday when cars and trucks were parked all the way to the cotton patch. I could almost hear the rhythmic beat of their voices echoing above the steeple.

Now the familiar row of gray tenant houses began. Even at that young age, I knew the occupants by name. Ella and Cleve lived in the first house. Aaron and Cora lived next door. Behind them lived Buster and Mattie. I could feel the warm safety of the only world I had ever known. The wide cypress boards proudly bore watermarks from the flood of 1927.

Now the road turned to meet the moss-covered water. A welcomed shade stretched across my path and the dust under my bare feet was suddenly cool and soft as velvet. The wide trunks of the tall cypress trees stood in the green slime where turtles rested lazily on rotting logs and water moccasins lurked beneath cool waters. For awhile we had a cook who was part Indian, and she told me there was an alligator in there. She said she could hear him lashing about in the night.

I was soon in front of Adeline's house, which was always bright in the summertime, with moss blooming in pots on her front porch. Then I could see Roxie's house on the ridge by our house, but there would be no tea parties today. On this hot afternoon, Roxie was nowhere in sight.

I was running now. I was almost there. I hurried up the path to our small white clapboard house with the screened porch across the front. I turned to see the black man coming up the road behind me. For the first time, I acknowledged his presence with a smile and a big wave. He had stayed with me all of the way. It only seemed right that I should share the joy of my victory with him.

I threw open the front screen door. It slammed shut with a pop as I plunged right into the living room and found myself in the midst of the bridge party. Among the strange faces, I located my mother. The stunned ladies saw my dusty feet and my red face as I buried myself in my mother's arms.

In a greatly controlled "company" voice, Mama asked, "My goodness, where did you come from? Who brought you home?"

She ran to the door looking for an automobile, but only saw the kind black gentleman turning to leave. She called for him to wait. He stopped and took off his Sunday brown felt hat that had a wide brim and grograin band. "Miz Mary," he explained, "I met yo' girl right outside town. She be's so little to be walkin' that long way by herself."

Mama thanked him over and over again and told him she would take him back into town if he could wait a little while. She turned back to her guests, trying to recapture her composure. The ladies spoke of the amazing feat and laughed as I saw Mama trying to hide her anger. When they were gone, she scolded me for coming across that highway and for not telling Carrie's maid, but then she hugged me and everything was all right again. Mama and I both knew it was just something I had to do.

Dr. Wilson

HIS ROUND FACE seemed much too large for the body of this small man wearing wire-rimmed glasses. A thin tuft of gray hair was combed across the top of his bald head. Our town physician wore black high top shoes with large round toes and a worn gray suit with a starched white shirt and tie. He was the only Republican in town.

His square brick office space was conveniently located behind the drugstore. His name was printed in gold letters on a small black sign hanging over the screen door leading into the two rooms with bare concrete floors. A worn black leather chair stood surrounded by shelves with narrow slots for a variety of glasses, lenses, and frames. In the back room was a leather-covered table where patients would lie down to be diagnosed. When I went to boarding school and came here for my physical exam, he stood me in one room and shouted to me from the other in order to test my hearing. Together we filled out my papers and he checked off the childhood diseases with efficient accuracy, for he had diagnosed most of these illnesses.

It is difficult to imagine now how helpless we were so far in the country. My sister, Martha Ann, died of scarlet fever at age four, before I was born. There were no antibiotics. She died the day after she became ill. I am sure my parents must have been frightened when I ended up with the same disease several years later. I spent almost my entire second grade in the hospital with ear complications. I took the brand new Sulfa drug that came in powdered form and was dissolved in a tablespoon full of water. I wish sometimes that I could go back and apologize to the nurse who administered my first dose without explaining the process adequately. I don't know why, maybe I was a little angry because I had been sick so long, but I spit the miracle cure all over her starched white uniform, which made her very unhappy.

My mother said that Dr. Wilson was an "eclectic." That meant that he never actually went to a medical college, but we had great confidence in this kind gentleman who brought his 70-year-old wife as a bride to our small town. He had celebrated his 50th anniversary with his first wife. When she died, he returned to his hometown to marry his childhood sweetheart, who had waited for him all of those years.

Dr. Wilson prescribed quinine for most all illnesses. With the abundance of mosquitoes in the area, he felt malaria to be the most likely candidate. His true expertise lay in his good common sense and ability to listen. The bright little eyes reminded me of the age old description of St. Nick: "His eyes how they twinkled." When he came to our house, he gathered us children at his feet and began his Paul Bunyan tales that fascinated us for hours.

Once I awoke with such a severe "crick" in my neck that I could not move. Our family's history of polio and rheumatic fever prompted my father to stop by Dr. Wilson's office when he went to town to get the mail. We had no telephone, nor did most of his patients. He followed my Dad back to our house in his battered old Hudson automobile and rushed up our front lawn with urgency.

He sat on my bed and talked for a moment. He then took me in his arms ever so carefully and sat my feet down on the big sturdy toes of his high top shoes. Together, we walked slowly across the living room floor with my parents watching nervously. He explained as he went back and forth together, that a "cold had settled in my neck" and that he was "working out the kinks." Sure enough, as I moved about with the gentle assurance of his arms, the frightening stiffness began to disappear. He sat there with my parents for some time, having a cup of coffee and Mother's latest cake. No one ever left our house without being fed in some way, and Dr. Wilson seldom seemed to be in a hurry. That was all part of the cure.

Years later, when I brought my fiancé home for the weekend, we met Dr. Wilson coming out of church. He stopped while his eyes scanned the body of my "intended" from head to toe. He then reached out and took his arm to squeeze it right below the shoulder as though he were conducting a physical examination. "Well, he seems to be in pretty good shape," he commented without emotion. Satisfied with his evaluation, he turned to walk away.

He came to our wedding and the reception in the back yard among Mama's pink day lilies. He was 90 years old, and it was the last social event he ever attended.

The Boarding House

MRS. DAVENPORT'S BOARDING house was in the middle of the "residential" section of our town on the cool quiet street near the schoolyard. A large porch wrapped around the two-story wooden dwelling that had not been painted in years. "Ole Dr. Davenport," as everyone called him, had passed away a long time ago. Somehow it was difficult to imagine Mrs. Davenport with a husband. She was a very independent and self-sufficient lady.

Every time I saw her, she was standing before the large iron range in her kitchen, stirring the steaming pans. In the heat, her black curly hair formed ringlets around her small wrinkled face. The lines radiating from her tiny puckish mouth formed a permanent smile. Her eyes blinked with a nervous twitch when she spoke in a rapid patter without any teeth. With incredible speed her petite body raced from the stove to the table, answering the needs of those she fed.

A long table covered in oilcloth stretched the length of the kitchen. It was always set and ready for the next meal. In a central cluster stood the vinegar set, salt, pepper, a large bottle of ketchup and Worchester Sauce. The generosity of her fare was overwhelming. She daily prepared mashed potatoes, baked potatoes, and potatoes au gratin with her fried chicken, country fried steak, or meat loaf — each richly endowed with gravy. There were biscuits, cornbread, and most likely a peach cobbler and rice pudding with raisins.

Since our school had no lunchroom facilities, students who lived in town went home and the rest of us brought a cold lunch. After my bout with scarlet fever, I sometimes I sat at Mrs. Davenport's noonday table. Mother thought I needed a hot meal on the coldest days, and it was too far to drive the two miles back home. On those days my mother gave me a 50-cent piece to give to Mrs. Davenport, who quickly tucked it into her apron pocket while reciting the menu for the day.

I don't remember much about the boarders who gathered around Mrs. Davenport's kitchen table, but most of them were old men. They sauntered in to find their usual seat, seldom bothering to exchange pleasantries. Whenever I went there, I walked quickly to the kitchen, hurrying past the dark mysterious rooms and the gloomy red velvet parlor where lace draperies were always drawn.

The only time I ever saw her outside the walls of her spacious kitchen was at church, which she attended every Sunday morning with her only child, Katherine. They sat together on the first row, for Katherine was the church secretary. During the hymns, Katherine turned around and counted heads; then later she gave her attendance report and slid the number cards into the wooden board at the front of the small sanctuary.

Every weekday, Katherine rode in a carpool to Little Rock to work in an office. I happened to ride in the same carpool with her when I went to Little Rock High School in the tenth grade. There was a high school in England, Arkansas, just four miles from Keo, but I could not get the courses there that I would need for college. This seemed to be a good solution. Every morning by 5:30 a.m., my father drove me from the farm to Keo and left me at Hiram Neal's filling station on the highway. Mr. Neal put nickels in the pinball machine to entertain me until my ride from England arrived to pick up Katherine and me.

Katherine and I sat together in the crowded back seat of that smoke-filled car, which was otherwise occupied by men going to their jobs in town. In her black suede platform shoes with the ankle straps, she seemed much taller than her mother, but she was so thin that her pelvic bones protruded beyond her stomach. Long after it was fashionable, she did her hair in a pompadour similar to the coiffeurs in World War II movies. She always wore a hat to church.

There was a wistful sadness in Katherine's drawn, dark face. Once, I asked my mother why her name was different from her mother's. She said Katherine had been married but her husband was never around. Katherine and her mother continued to live in the big house alone after the boarders had ceased to come, but Mrs. Davenport was busy cooking in that kitchen until the day she died.

After I went away to boarding school, Katherine continued to ride that same carpool every day. Not long after her mother's death, Katherine's name appeared in all of the Little Rock papers. It seems that one afternoon after work, she walked past the bus station to the center of the bridge spanning the Arkansas River in downtown Little Rock and jumped off. No one could believe it. Katherine had always been so dependable.

Mr. Bowden

MR. BOWDEN WAS my father's bookkeeper at the cotton gin office. When he spoke, he had to talk around the cigar that was permanently lodged between his teeth. I don't ever remember him starting out with a fresh one. It always seemed to be short and worn almost to the end, trapped in the corner of his lips as he pored over the thick ledger books with little green lines that separated his neat, precise figures. They say his children were grown before he went back to Draughon's Business School in Little Rock to get his degree in accounting.

He and his wife lived in a neat house down the street from the drugstore. My father had given it to him several years before. He spoke with great respect of "Virgie," who was the mother of his five children. She chewed tobacco, wore her gray hair twisted at the top of her head, and spent most of her time around the quilting frame that filled her living room.

Daddy's check register was almost illegible to anyone except Mr. Bowden. In his relentless effort to keep impeccable records, he patiently pursued the illusive pieces of paper that my father carelessly stuffed in his pockets. His attempts were quite difficult in the turbulent routine of a cotton gin, yet I never heard Mr. Bowden raise his voice. When the cotton wagons rolled across the scales at harvest time, no one questioned the accuracy of his figures.

When I was growing up there was no telephone at our house, but there was one at the gin office that Mr. Bowden answered. It was the only time he removed the cigar from his mouth. On the white painted wall beside it were important telephone numbers and any messages that anyone in the family may have received. The first time a young man called from Little Rock to ask me for a date, Mr. Bowden carefully relayed the message by pointing at the wall where he had carefully written the telephone number for me.

One summer, after I had graduated from college, I went to work at the gin. Mr. Bowden was to teach me to keep the books. He sat me down in my father's chair in front of his desk and began the lesson: accounts receivable, profits, expenses—the figures were spinning in my head. He quietly went over the system until I understood the relatively simple process. Somehow, it wasn't so bad asking Mr. Bowden the questions that arose in the mind of an English major. His lips curled around that ever-present cigar in an effort to hold back a grin when I asked why I couldn't put shoeing the horses under "repair." It seemed logical to me.

After a while, he trusted me enough to take a walk around the gin yard while I worked. On one hot summer day, I was poring over the bank statement when I heard him return. I looked up to see him walking slowly toward me, a strange look on his face.

"Now, I don't want to alarm you any," he said. "There's really no reason to panic. We have to stay calm. Now, don't get scared or anything, but I think the seed house is on fire. You may want to go look for yourself before we call the fire department down at England. They're awfully nice. I had to call them once before."

Trying to reconcile his slow manner with the context of his words, I flew past him and out the door to find the seed house in flames. I rushed back and nervously dialed a number that he had waiting for me when I returned.

The fire truck came screaming into town with its siren at full blast. The owner of the filling station and the general store came to help. There was more action than anyone had seen at the gin since the last harvest. Through it all, Mr. Bowden stood quietly, observing with a cool indifference the drama around us.

The flames were smothered before it spread, and the firemen started back to England after they had checked for smoldering fiber. The town's citizens, who had come out of both curiosity and an eagerness to help, drifted back home. Mr. Bowden and I were left alone with the lingering smell of roasted cottonseed.

He went back to his figures as though nothing had happened, while I paced nervously, peering out the doorway toward the ruined seed house. Without looking up from his ledgers, he said, "A thing like that is kinda unsettling, but it could've been worse. We best call the insurance people down at Pine Bluff and see if they want to come by and look at the damage. Your father will be back in the morning and that is the first thing he will ask."

I looked down at his hand as he lifted his pen to fit the numbers into the tiny squares on the green sheet before him, and for the first time saw that it was shaking.

Gene

ENE DID NOT visit often, for he lived in Wyoming and that was a long way from our farm in Arkansas. He was at least 10 years older than any of us and by far our favorite cousin. He spoke with a Midwestern accent in a soft, unhurried voice, as though he had all of the time in the world. He carried a pack of Camel cigarettes in his shirt pocket and was the only person I had ever known who wore real cowboy boots.

Gene's visits were in the summer, when we were not in school. He had long ago established a ritual that he faithfully observed when he came to our house. The days on the farm would be unbearably hot, so we waited for the night when the work was finished, the dishes were washed, and the adults were sitting on the front porch talking in a steady, unintelligible hum about things that never interested us children.

This is when Gene would take us back into the kitchen and get out the big iron skillet to make a batch of fudge. First, he piled up a mound of white sugar in the black pan, mixed enough cocoa to turn the grainy mixture brown, added two cups of milk and began the cooking process. Then he lifted me up to the counter top so that I, being the youngest one, would not miss any of the rites of this ceremony. We watched the dark liquid begin to bubble, sending forth the heavenly essence of chocolate.

It was time to begin Gene's testing procedure. He dribbled a tiny amount of the bubbling syrup into a teacup filled with cold water. With the first try, the small brown drop exploded and muddied the clear water. "Nope, it's not ready yet. Just hold your horses. We gotta give it time," he would say.

We watched with great interest as he repeated the process. We knew that when the drop of simmering fudge hit the water and stayed firm in one round ball, our fudge was done. Gene removed the pan from the stove and dropped a large spoonful of butter into the steaming pan. "Now, we'll have to wait until that cools." Then, he stood in the harsh kitchen light and talked. He told us about his school and how he rode horses across the rolling hills in Wyoming. He told us that the next summer, when he was 18, he was going to work with some archaeologists during his vacation. He would camp out for weeks in the desolate countryside and search for bones and fossils.

Our cousin Gene

As he talked, he tested the fudge and announced that it was time to begin the beating. We each took our turn until our arms ached and Gene took the spoon. We heard the sticky mass pop as he whipped with experienced hands. Then, with precise timing, he quickly poured the creamy fudge into the buttered platter, discreetly leaving a fair amount in the pan. That's when we got our first taste. He gave each one of us a spoon and we scraped and licked until the pan was clean.

Then our cousin took a wet knife and sliced neat squares of candy. While we guarded this delight, he went up into the attic to find our cotton quilt. It was the one Mother had designated as being old enough to spread outside in the grass. Carrying the plate of fudge and the quilt, we walked past the adults into the front yard. The stars were out and the crickets droned. We spread the pallet on the cool grass and the four of us lay on our backs so that we could see the stars. Gene showed us the "Big Dipper," the "Milky Way" and the brightest star of all.

He would say, "That is called the Evening Star. You don't ever have to be afraid because that one is always watching over you. Make a wish," he added with great urgency as though its gleaming light would disappear if we waited.

When we were quiet, Gene began to tell his ghost stories. We scooted closer to him when his words grew louder, rising with fervor to his final ending. Then he shouted something like, "Gotcha!" or "He ate them all up!" At the "scariest" part, he folded us all in his arms at once, laughing as we dissolved into giggles.

On December 7, 1941, the Japanese bombed Pearl Harbor. That summer our aunt wrote us that Gene had joined the Marines. He missed coming to our house that year. On November 20, 1943, Admiral Nimitz sent his forces into the Gilbert Islands. The Second Marine Division pushed ashore on a tiny island called Tarawa that was better fortified by the Japanese than the US Marines had ever expected. The coral reef, worn by sea and wind, had become a sandy beach with nothing on it but a few coconuts and screw pine. The atoll was secured four days later leaving 950 dead Marines.

That Christmas night a relative drove from town out to our house to deliver a message to our parents. They talked in whispers, but we heard Gene's name. We drove the 26 miles to Little Rock in silence, not daring to speak. Ignoring the bright Christmas lights and decorations, our father took us to the nearly deserted movie house on Main Street. He gave us money for our tickets and left us with plenty of nickels to buy Milk Duds and popcorn while he and Mother visited members of Gene's family. We had watched the movie *Robin Hood* with Errol Flynn twice when our parents finally came back for us. We rode home down the dark highway listening to the solemn announcement by our father.

Gene had only been in the Marines a few months when he landed on the foreign beach with the first batch of troops. As soon as we got home, we hurried to the blue *World Book* encyclopedias that lined our living room bookshelf and found a map of the Pacific Ocean. In the dim Delco battery light we sat staring on the page at the tiny dot marked Tarawa.

That evening, when I climbed between the covers, my whole body shook with fear. I thought about the black and white newsreels of soldiers storming the shores and falling on that strange beach so far from home. I could not leave Gene in that place. I crept out of bed and kneeled by the window. Looking up into the sky, I searched for our lucky star. It was there, just as he promised it always would be. I stared at its twinkling light a long time, remembering those summer nights, the ghost stories and how safe we felt on that old quilt in the front yard with Gene.

Maybe dying was like the ending to one of Gene's stories. Maybe that's when God gathers us in his arms and we're not frightened any more. It was good to imagine Gene warm and safe like that. For a moment I thought I could hear him laughing in this, the scariest part of all.

Henrietta

A NARROW DAM OF hard clay led across the water to Henrietta's house. I felt excited by the adventure of passing through the dark tunnel of willow trees to reach her house. Long ago my Dad had taken me to meet her. I was sure that as a child, he had also made the journey to visit her. Surrounded by discarded enamel kitchen vessels filled with red verbena, prince feathers, and blooming moss, she sat on her porch in a cane chair, watching the only entrance to her world.

Her ankle-length flannel skirt touched sturdy high top shoes that were laced over heavy cotton stockings. A long sleeve blouse, patched and repaired with hand stitches, hung loosely over a layer of cotton underwear. She wore the same archaic clothes winter and summer. Some said that she had been burned as a child for the only glimpse of her black skin, revealed large areas of pink splotches on her face and hands. I found myself wondering at the strange parts of her skin that were just like mine with freckles sprinkled across them. Her gray steel wool hair was parted in neat little squares with a braid in the center of each.

In the afternoons, toting her own chair, fishing pole, and a bucket, Adeline walked down to the shade of the cypress trees on the bayou. She arranged the layers of her long skirt around her, put on her immense straw hat, and began to fish. She raised her long cane pole above her head and thrust it forward, flinging the line out into the bayou where the round cork settled on the black waters. She seemed to know which bush or waterlogged stump sheltered the catfish. When the cork began to bob up and down and skim across the water, her experienced hands pulled up the line to expose the brilliant white belly of a fish with long whiskers like a kitten. Henrietta's jaw was set firmly as she wrested the sharp hook free from the gaping mouth, plopped the fish down into the bucket of water beside her chair, and reached for the tin can filled with squirming bait to begin the process all over again.

Most mornings I could find Henrietta on her porch. I tied the leather rein of my horse to one of the post that supported her shingled roof, and sat on the steps at her feet to talk. She asked me about school and about my family. I found myself telling her everything that was going though my mind at that particular stage of my life. She listened and observed, then offered her blunt advice in that husky voice. There was something regal about Henrietta, long ensconced in her high back cane chair.

Henrietta always offered me a drink from the pump in her front yard. Hobbling down the front steps, she came to assist me in the priming. She filled a dipper from a bucket of water near by and poured it into the pitcher of the pump as she pushed the handle up and down. Using my tight fingers as a container, I drank the cool clear water as it erupted in my hands. After many years, the memory of its fresh clean taste lingers.

The Red Purse

A S I SLAMMED the door of my Dad's mud spattered truck, a bell tolled from the steeple rising over the flaking white washed schoolhouse. Hurrying inside, I could smell fresh oil on the wide planked floors meant to absorb the coal dust filtering from iron stoves in the center of each classroom. I was eight years old and it was 1940.

Walking down the hall, my hand reached inside the pocket of my woolen snowsuit. My fingers slid across the smooth leather coin purse and the cold metal tracks of its zipper. Inside was a carefully folded new dollar bill.

My father had taken me around the farm with him the Saturday before so that he could talk with me alone, "You know you're going to be nine this April? It's about time that you had your own allowance. Your mother and I think that it would be good for you to have a hot lunch some days at school. You could walk down to Mr. Leake's drugstore or maybe Mrs. Davenport's boarding house. I want you to learn to manage your own money and maybe you can save some too. Your brothers didn't get their allowance until they were 12, but I think you're ready for that kind of responsibility. We'll start on Monday. Let's try one dollar a week."

This morning my father had called me into his bedroom. Reaching into the top dresser drawer where he kept all of his treasures, he pulled out the dollar bill and a small red leather change purse. "Now, here's something for you to carry it in. Remember, it's yours to manage."

On this Monday morning I was elated by my new responsibility as I hurried though the large double doors that led past Mr. Ashcraft's office into the third grade room. Class had not yet begun. A small group of students mingled between the rows of desks that were bolted to the black floor. Fellow and Thurmond stood beside the teacher's desk comparing their latest marble acquisitions. Fellow's round face was shining from the morning scrub. His blond hair, combed back with water, would fall carelessly about his face by noon. The large sized corduroy pants were gathered around his waist by a black leather belt. His white shirt was carefully starched and ironed by his mother, who never seemed to leave their large rambling house adjoining the school property. When I was allowed to ride our Shetland Pony "Little Bits", cutting though the back field and avoiding the road to our house, Fellow let me tie her up in his front yard. Sometimes, when we played marbles on the hard ground in circles drawn in the dust, he let me use his best "aggie" for luck.

Thurmond was smaller than the other fourth graders, but we all knew he was 14. Blue striped overall, like the ones that locomotive engineers wear, hung loosely from his thin shoulders. His chest was rounded from the air hunger that had plagued him since his birth. His fingers were grotesquely large at their ends with the bluish purple color that had labeled him a "blue baby." He told us proudly about the leak in his heart. Sometimes, I saw him downtown smoking a cigarette and spitting into the street right alongside the older boys in town. Miss Julia always said that Thurmond was talented. His drawings were by far the best in the class when they were displayed on colored construction paper along the walls. He built his own pencil box and was always carrying something ingenious in his pocket that he had invented.

Brother and Sister were twins. Their real names were Violus and Varlan. Her bright freckled face was crowned by two braids, so tight that they must have made her head ache. Her family lived on our place and she was my good friend. Pat hurried in from the cloakroom carrying two felt erasers she had just pounded together outside the backdoor as part of her chores as monitor for the week. Her black wool coat was covered in chalk dust as she hurried inside with heavy steps that shook the floor as she walked.

Charlene's sun-bleached hair was cut in bangs across her forehead, short and straight above her ears, and sheared like a boy in the back. She shivered in a cotton print dress and brown laced shoes that were still damp from the 2-mile walk into town that morning. Her name had the most "Xs" for absences in Miss Julia's roll book and the least number of checks on the orange Ipana toothpaste and Lifebuoy soap chart that hung beside the blackboard. We were to put a cross in one of the little squares if we had brushed our teeth and washed our hands that morning.

At the beginning of the year, her mother had come to school with Charlene to hear her "recitations." All day she sat on the back row with the youngest of her eight children in her arms. Her gray hair was pulled back in a ball on top of her head. Her brown wrinkled face was without expression and far too weathered and worn for her age. When the baby began to cry, she unbuttoned the front of her faded dress and started to nurse. Miss Julia continued as though nothing unusual was going on in the back of her classroom.

That morning, I went straight to the cloakroom and sat on the floor trying to pull off the hated woolen leggings that were too hot to wear inside all day. As Sister wandered in to find me, there was a thump on the floor when the coin purse slipped from my pocket. As I proudly showed it to my best friend, most of the small class crowded into the cloakroom to see my new possession. When Miss Julia called us back to our desks, I carefully tucked it back into my coat pocket.

Scooting into the hard wooden seat that curved to fit my back, I rubbed my hand over the smooth desk and followed the carved lines in its surface which spelled out names of students from long ago who were grown ups now. I recognized some of them. It was fun to imagine what they were like in the fourth grade. I reached underneath to the books stacked in the shelf below and felt the familiar worn cover of a spelling book. Together we began to read the new words aloud. Repetition was essential. Every word was repeated just as we went over the subtraction and multiplications cards over and over again.

The morning passed slowly as I gazed out on this gloomy February day though pane windows decorated with paper patterned snowflakes and black silhouettes of Lincoln and Washington. Their 12th and 22nd February birth dates were firmly planted in my mind as we heard again the stories every year of these revered presidents.

The memory of that whole day is dim and gray, like an old black and white movie except for one stroke of color – the Valentine box. Friday would be the long awaited holiday. Today we were supposed to vote for two students to decorate the Valentine's Day box. It would be a great honor. I shuffled in my seat trying to hold back the excitement, hoping that I would be chosen.

As I glanced at the round hatbox on the floor behind the teacher's desk, I imagined decorating it with red and white crepe paper. I could almost feel the ridged surface between my fingers as I pulled it apart to make little bubbles and gather it into a billowing red skirt around the circular opening of the box. By now we were turning the pages of our large thin geography book with colored maps of far away places. The vision of the lovely box that would hold our Valentine's cards made it impossible to concentrate on places too far away to understand.

"All right, children, we'll stop here for recess, but before we do, could we elect those two who will be responsible for our Valentine Box? Write your choices on a small piece of tablet paper and I will collect them."

Miss Julia's slender young body moved down the aisle holding a cardboard pencil box while each child dropped his or her selection inside. She sat down at her desk stacking the uneven slips of paper in separate piles. Finally, she looked up at me and announced, "It looks as though you and Thurmond will be in charge of the Valentine box this year."

I rushed to the desk with Thurmond while others gathered around us to plan the box for the special day. Lida Sue had to tell us what she had done last year and Fellow offered to bring his mother's homemade flour and water paste. With all of the excitement, recess was unusually long. It seemed to take forever to get us all seated at our desks. The back door slammed as someone returned from the outdoor facilities marked, "Boys" and "Girls," but I never looked to see who it was.

Mrs. Julia decided to read us a story rather than begin our usual multiplication tables. The big bell tolled again and it was time for lunch. Most of the students walked to their homes close to school. A few reached inside their desk for a brown sack or lard bucket filled with cold biscuits, meat and thick tea cookies, mostly what was left over from the supper table the night before. I hurried to get my coat and walk the few blocks downtown to buy my lunch with my own money at Mr. Leake's drugstore. As I reached in my pocket for the treasured purse, the empty flannel lining forced me to try the second pocket, but it wasn't there either. My cry from the cloakroom brought the remaining classmates squeezing into the small area with Miss Julia.

"Now, that's all right, I'm sure we will find it," she said.

With no success, Miss Julia disappeared down the hall to the principal's office and we sat silently waiting in the room for a long time. I stared straight ahead, but by mind raced over each face in the room trying to determine who had deceived me.

I remembered once when we watched the boys gather around their usual circle drawn in the dust, Fellow ignored the time-honored male tradition and loaned me his favorite "aggie" to play a game of marbles with them. I thought about the doll bed made from rough lumber that Thurmond had built for me. I could feel the hard shiny jacks in my hand as Charlie May and I played a game on the school steps. Jeanine sometimes asked me to come home with her for lunch when her family gathered around the big round table to have a bowl of cooked rice with sweet milk and sugar. I was remembering how I told Sister my best-kept secrets as we seesawed up and down on a board balanced across the log in her back yard near my house.

My thoughts were interrupted as Miss Julia returned with the principal. He was a devoted, intense man with advanced ideas on education. If a child were gifted, he sacrificed his own time to work with them on an individual basis. His temper, however, could change his mood like an explosion. Sometimes he stood before the entire school during morning chapel and entertained us by making his face into terrible contortions of anger, sadness, happiness, and stupidity. Though the high school students laughed, I stared in horror and fear. Today, the deep lines of his face were red with rage as he spoke,

"Now, we don't stand for stealing in this school. One of you took the money. 'Thou shalt not steal!' It is a sin to take anything that does not belong to you. I want it returned. We're going back to the cloakroom to search everyone's things right now."

He stormed past our desk into the narrow backroom with Miss Julia close behind wearing her worried expression. The fourth grade students in the class sat still, fearing the impending consequences of the search in progress. Sometimes a teacher disappeared with a student into the inner sanctum of the cloakroom. It was always a boy. We all listened for the terrible thud of the paddle against flesh. Sometimes the victim re-appeared flushed but stoically silent. At other times, a scream preceded a sobbing exit from the intimidating room. We never minded it quite as much when Miss Julia marched a classmate back there and whispered quietly to him. Today the principal returned alone, pointing an accusing finger, "I did not find that money, but I will. A thief will be found out!"

The warm magic of the Valentine box was gone. I hated the money and what it had done to this special day. Sister offered me one of her cold biscuits and we waited quietly for the others to return from lunch.

After a long afternoon, the big bell finally rang at 3 p.m. The small group of students disappeared quickly and I was left struggling trying to pull the worrisome snowsuit pants over my shoes. I began to sweat in the hot jacket. My heart thumped so loudly that I knew Miss Julia could hear it from the front of the classroom. Turning quickly, I slipped out the back door and ran to the street where I saw my father's familiar truck waiting for me. I longed for the safety of its sanctuary. I would never know who took the money but I learned that day how little it mattered.

Mrs. Wilbanks

MRS. WILBANKS HAD been my mother's sixth grade teacher and her exceptional talents in her lifelong profession were well known. When our town's supply of teachers began to dwindle as their servicemen husbands took them away to new locations, my mother decided that it was time to place me under the expert tutelage of Mrs. Wilbanks in the town of England, four miles away.

Mrs. Wilbanks was a small, lady but her strength was heard in her quick bold steps echoing down the hall. The excessive white powder failed to hide the massive wrinkles in her face, but her eyes were like fire and her thick glasses magnified their power. No one crossed Mrs. Wilbanks.

Disobeying her was never a question. She had taught so many years that her days were like clockwork. We memorized our multiplication tables and recited them over and over again until we got them right. There was no slipping by. If we were weak in a subject, she would find us out. We could never hide our deficiencies. When we had the mathematical basics, she allowed us to do "word problems."

"If you travel so many miles an hour and have so many miles to go then how long would it take to get there?" We were given more and more of these hypothetical situations until we could apply this knowledge to our lives. The same was true for English. We were made to diagram sentence after sentence until we were able to compose our own with the proper structure.

Johnny and Tony sat on the back row and giggled only the first day. After that there were no behavior problems. Mrs. Wilbanks' discipline was old-fashioned, stern, and effective. We had to write pages of "I will nots" or "I wills," do extra lessons, or stay after school, but mostly, it only took one of her stern looks to defer any offenders.

Mrs. Wilbanks' classroom was in the same dark sturdy two-story brick building where my mother had come to school. The gloomy hallways were filled with more students than I had previously seen in one place. It was all strange and different to me, but my mother had told me that to be in Mrs. Wilbanks' class was an honor and privilege. She was right. In all my academic pursuits, I had reason to thank Mrs. Wilbanks for making my tasks easier.

Joy

One of the best parts of going to junior high school in England, was being in class everyday with my very first "for life" friend, Joy. I remember her walking in strong sure strides with those beautiful chestnut braids bouncing down her back almost to her waist. She was the youngest of eight children. Her four sisters were all grown and married. Joy claimed they would not allow her to cut her hair. I could never understand why she would want to do such a thing, but Joy had a mind of her own. By the time we had our sixth grade graduation pictures made, she had a new haircut.

She lived in a big two-story house with her two older brothers in the small town where I went to school. Since I lived out in the county, I would often spend the night with her. It was a wonderful place, filled with the bustle of a large family coming and going. Through her older sisters she acquired knowledge beyond the limits of our small town and was quite sophisticated, I thought. She knew all of the latest fashions and had a natural "flair" in the clothes she wore.

Joy introduced me to my first Broadway show on her sister's phonograph album *Oklahoma*. Her aunt was the local booking agent for Little Rock's concerts and stage shows at the municipal auditorium. Our parents would often drive us the 20 miles to the city to hear current stage celebrities like the opera star, Risë Stevens, and the noted pianist, Eugene List. Joy's aunt would introduce them to us and let us get their autographs. She acquired two signed glossy prints for us of Ronald Reagan, which we both proudly set on our dressers. She always knew the latest on all of the movie stars.

I mostly remember our year together in the sixth grade under Mrs. Wilbanks. My good friend was left-handed, and I could see her struggling to find a comfortable position on her small cramped desk. She did not particularly enjoy schoolwork, and I don't ever remember her letting the stress of homework spoil her day. She always seemed to have the "big picture" and small things did not crowd her thoughts.

Her mother was a Girl Scout leader, so we both went to Girl Scout camp. Jointly, we survived the discipline of peeling potatoes and cleaning latrines. Together, we discovered boys and suffered the agony of our first parties, playing spin the bottle, and vying for drugstore dates. She never took the pursuit of boys very seriously. At this early age, she was incredibly level headed and kept her sense of humor about it all.

It was about this time that she lost her oldest brother in a tragic cotton gin accident. Somehow she was always strong enough to meet the challenges that would follow when she lost her elderly parents, two husbands, and an older sister. Whenever I would come to console her, she ended up consoling me. She accepted these losses with the great strength and faith that we all came to expect of her.

After junior high, our paths separated when I went away to boarding school. When college came, she headed for Texas and SMU. She was perfectly suited for Texas, for there was not an ounce of pretense in her body. I was in her wedding, and she was in mine. Years later, she came all of the way from Texas to attend my daughter's wedding. When the bride and groom had sped away and the last guest had disappeared, I suddenly felt devastated. My husband had taken some of the out of town visitors to their hotels. I went up to the dressing room where the wedding gown lay crumpled in a heap on the floor, and there was my loyal friend waiting for me. We rode home together in the big limousine and giggled all the way. She knew how to make the best of every moment.

Even though her parents were more like grandparents, Joy was patient and held great respect for them. Her mother was a tall lady, kind and soft-spoken. She seemed to make few demands on Joy. There was no need. Values, standards, and principles were engrained in the household. Her father had taught my mother in the Methodist Sunday school and God's words ruled his life and that of his children. Her father lived much longer than her mother, but he seemed to shrink with every year. He looked a little like the pictures of Mahatma Ghandi, but he had a wonderful laugh. She told me about taking him to the beach in his final days. Since walking was so difficult for him, she picked up his small body and carried him down to the seashore.

In the past few years, most of our contact has been by telephone or postcards. Whether she was in Dallas, Wyoming, or on a trip to Europe, we stayed in touch with each other. We talked of children and later grandchildren. She continued to keep me current with all the latest and the best. She gave me a wonderful Dallas cookbook and the poppy seed dressing recipe from the Neiman Marcus tearoom. The handwritten instructions (smudged with a little oil and sugar) are tucked safely in my recipe box. It's always been nice to go back and find her handwriting there.

When I was happy and excited, I couldn't wait to share it with her. When I was sad, I needed her strong slow reassuring voice, saying "Well, Sis" followed always by something positive.

As a child she had rheumatic fever and later in life, heart by-pass surgery. Her beautiful chestnut hair turned gray, but she remained stylish and youthful wearing her acquired blond hair with a short "pageboy" cut. She could never be old.

She gave me my first taste of music and art. She found the best in all things. She knew the finest, yet she kept her feet firmly on the ground. She always ended her telephone call with, "I love you." Her voice echoes in my ears sometimes when I try to fathom the reality of her death. She was my life-time friend. She was the gold standard of what that means.

The Storm

I WAS IN THE first grade that early spring day when a warm wind whistled around the corners of the schoolhouse, howling as though it were trying to tell us something. The minutes edged by until the three o'clock bell freed us to run outside in the blustery March afternoon.

My parents would be late coming to pick me up after school so I was to walk home with Jeanine French. We had decided during recess that this would be the day to take off our shoes and wade in the puddles in front of her house. The freezes and snows had left the only gravel road through town with wide potholes filled to the brim by recent rains. Every summer the county graded and filled the seasonal damage but for now, it was our playground.

Sissy in first day school dress

I remember feeling rather daring that day, for my mother hated for us to go barefoot. I never understood why she wanted to deny my brother and me the joys of sloshing around in the water,, feeling the coolness when we walked back upon the green grass in the front yard. It was a ritual, a sort of expression of independence and freedom. Today, my mother was driving Miss Echole to the beauty shop four miles away, and my daddy was in Lonoke, the county seat, at a Production Credit Association meeting.

We carefully placed our socks inside our lace-up brown shoes by the front door and ventured forth rather cautiously on tender feet. The day had been sticky, humid, and gloomy. The sky was getting darker and darker. I sensed danger as the light breeze grew to a blustering wind blowing across my face. I soon found myself fighting to keep my balance against its force. Mrs. French appeared on the front porch, holding back the screen door as she called, "You kids get yourselves into this house right now. A storm's coming!"

I grabbed my shoes as we passed through the door that slammed protectively behind me. I looked around the dark room of her modest home. It was filled with familiar faces that I had seen around town. I wasn't sure just who they were, but they all seemed to know me. I guess they were mostly friends and relatives of the French's. The postman's wife was hovering on one side with her sister and three relatives lined up in chairs against the wall, almost like a church meeting. No men were present this time of day. As I searched for a place to sit, a large lady in a flowered print dress with a white powered face, reeking of perfume, motioned me over to sit with her. She pulled me into her lap, holding me tight against her bosoms, with comforting words, "You poor little thing, now don't be scared!"

Suddenly, I could feel the wind grow stronger as the fragile dwelling shook against its force. The noise increased as it built to a thunderous roar, rattling against the tin roof. The ladies began to moan and cry.

"Bless your little heart, your Mama ain't here. Don't you worry none, we're going to take care of you if the Lord is willing. Praise the Lord...Lord keep us." Her words were echoed and they became a chant screaming against the howling winds. My mother had always made fun of those who were afraid of storms. She would laugh and say, "If God is going to take us there isn't a thing we can do about it. I am not going to crawl under a bed nor go down in one of those storm cellars where the snakes are more of a danger than the weather and I am not going around scared of death most of my life!"

I thought of her and wished she were here. I was more afraid of the moaning ladies than I was of the storm. I wanted very much to wrestle free of the fat arms and run. Then with a loud crash, a part of the roof blew off and water poured inside. Mrs. French hustled to get buckets and towels. With all of this confusion we failed to notice that it was suddenly very quiet. The wailing stopped, and we all sat in silence for a long time.

The persistent lady's vice-like grip was relaxed. I freed myself and ran toward the door. Mrs. French slowly opened it and peeked out, saying, "Nothin's been hit too hard out there, I don't think. Thank the Lord!"

The sky was a bright yellow – unlike anything I had ever seen. This eerie color hung over the town where tree branches lay across the road and pieces of tin had been thrown into the streets. We all stood on the porch, surveying the damage in silence, stunned by the awesome power of the storm. Then everyone set about the task of cleaning up and the laughter of relief came as they discussed how they might get the men to cover the hole in the roof before dark. They would tell about this day for many years, along with the often-repeated stories about the great flood of '27.

I saw my mother's car pull up out front, and she ran to me with an anxious urgency that had not anticipated. I had never once doubted that she would come or worried about her safety. Like the women of Proverbs, "She laughed at the time to come," and held us all together, but when I saw her worried face, I lost my courage and ran into her arms.

She called to Mrs. French, "Thanks for taking care of my child. I'm so glad you're all all right." My father and brothers were in the car. Gathered together in that four-door 1938 Chevrolet, we started home. It seemed as though nothing could harm us now. During the storm, a tree had blocked my Dad's road and he had to take a back route. Mama was precariously perched on an embankment beside the highway with the car rocking back and forth while Miss Echole sang every verse of "Shall We Gather at the River."

The boys were under the counter in Uncle Jimmie's brick store watching all the debris fly past the plate glass windows as though they were with

Dorothy and Toto in *The Wizard of Oz*. We were joking with the deep assurance that came with being together again when we saw a stranger, from the adjoining farm, walking alongside the road, trying to hail us down. "Mr. Morris, they say your house is done blowed away. It hit hard out here. 'Course, I ain't been all the way out there yet but that's what they say."

No one spoke a word as we drove past the newly plowed fields, desolate and bare in this early spring rain, awaiting the seeds that would bring new life. No matter what happened at school or church or in Little Rock or the world, we could come home. We felt superior and protected, as though we didn't have to go by the same rules as everyone else, until now. Our minds were racing through the possibilities awaiting us. My grandfather had built the small sturdy house on the hill many years ago. Green shutters framed the pane windows and a screen porch stretched across the front. A large oak tree towered above its shingled roof and held our bag swing. Two weeping willows dropped their graceful branches to touch the lawn. My room was on the front closest to the bayou.

I thought of the green living room with its starched white organdy curtains blowing in the violent wind and the fragile French glass doors going into the company dining room. Most of all, I thought about the kitchen, the big iron stove, its warmth and the talks we had while Mother cooked supper.

In my mind, I went over every detail of our house, seeing it more clearly than ever before, trying to imagine how it would look now.

Mother broke the silence, "William, I suppose Annie would let us stay with her until morning." No one answered the terrible thought of our being dependent on my Dad's sister. We had never been dependent on anyone except each other. My heart was beating so fast I could scarcely breath. We had to pass the bayou and the tall trees before we would see our house that sat on a hill around the bend. We strained our necks to get a better view, for we all knew exactly at what point it would come into sight. My brother cried first, "It's there; it's still there!"

The trees were lying down on their sides. The green and white awnings that protected the porch from the sun were torn into shreds. The rain had poured into the opened windows until the carpet was soaked, but the house was standing. We had no lights. The Delco battery system was out. Mother walked right past the havoc that the storm had wrought and started fixing supper by an old coal oil lantern. Somehow Mother going into the kitchen brought things back to normal. We gathered around a candlelit table and Daddy said his usual blessing,

"Lord, make us thankful for these and thy many blessings, Amen."

When we popped our heads up, ready to begin the meal, we saw that our mother's head remained bowed. She always had more to talk over with the Lord than the rest of us. We sat quietly while she finished.

We ate some Bonnie's Buttered Beef Steak, the first frozen food we had ever heard about. Mama had bought it at the new commercial freezer place down in England where she had taken Miss Echole to get her hair fixed. She told Daddy how nice it would be to rent a locker and freeze some of our vegetables, strawberries, and even pork sausage to have all year long. She was trying, but there were big gaps of silence that night around our table. We had a lot of thinking to do and our feelings were too strong to talk about just then.

Monday Is the Day We Wash the Clothes

AND TUESDAY IS the day we iron. That never changed except when it rained. Rain was the only event that would change the day of the week that Ella and Mattie did our washing.

Ella and Mattie were married to the two main tractor drivers on the place. They came every Monday morning up to a our house to wash the clothes in big tin tubs, rubbing the fabric up and down against the smooth rippled metal of wood framed washboards. The white sheets boiled in Borax to a brilliant white in a big black pot with a fire built underneath it. Later, in another pot, the white powder of Faultless starch was poured to form the milky hot liquid to make our cotton clothes crisp and keep their shape better.

The efforts of their morning labor were then hung with clothespins on the long stretch of wires that hung across our backyard on wooden poles. On these permanent clothes lines, the colored fabric blew in puffs and the sheets billowed like giant sails in the warm sunshine. About noontimes, the two black women with canvas clothes pin bags slung over their shoulders, went to gather the clean smelling piles of wrinkled cotton and carry them to the empty cook's house behind our garage.

There Ella and Mattie came Tuesday morning to do the ironing. I slipped out the back door and crawled up on the old iron bed with its abandoned mattress to hear the two gossip as they went about their task.

At first, wood was burned in the tin stove at the center of the room in order to heat the heavy triangular irons with handles that had to be held with hot pads. Later we acquired a smaller more modern round stove filled briquettes to do the job, distributing less heat in the ironing room on a summer morning.

I saw Mattie and Ella sprinkle droplets of water on each piece and crumple it in a ball to soften it for the ironing process. I watched as their steady hands moved the pointed edge of their crude iron into the gathers of a dress, into the sleeve of a blouse, or slide it straight down the front of my father's white shirt. I was fascinated as they worked their magic to make the crinkles smooth and crisp. When the iron cooled off, they would put it back on a small grill filled with briquettes and pick up another hot one to continue.

They talked and laughed and rested a while, making the ironing day go quickly. Sometimes, they brought the three-colored coconut candy to sell for their church. The chocolate, strawberry, and vanilla stripes in a cellophane package tasted just a little like soap, but nevertheless, I convinced my mother to give me a quarter to purchase their church fundraising product.

Sometimes, I begged to try to make the wrinkles go away and demonstrate my own ability. "Now, Miss Sissy, don't you go ruinin' your mother's best dress. Here, just try this here pillow case."

I held the heavy iron and pushed it forward and pulled it back lightly. "You have to push down a little too, honey; you may not be strong enough just yet! Now let me have it back, we got to get these clothes in the house before Mr. William comes home for supper."

We had one of the first electric washing machines, with the wringer on the top that had to be hand cranked as you ran a piece through it to squeeze out most of the moisture before it was hung on the line to dry. The modern world brought Clorox and spray starch, but it was not until the REA (Rural Electricity of Arkansas) came to the farm that we had electric irons and clothes dryers.

The smell of heat touching the starched cotton always reminds me of those summer days out in the cook's house. I still like to push the iron over fabric and smooth out the wrinkles. It is like making everything all right again. There is something satisfying about that.

The Watkins Man

THE WATKINS MAN who came each summer drove a Ford Sedan with the name of his company painted prominently on the side. Since horse-drawn wagons, Watkins had owned Owl Motor Company, a subsidiary of Ford Motors, in order to supply the transportation needs of its sales force. Piled on the back seat of his car, with his bulging worn brief case, were cartons of black pepper, cloves, cinnamon, cocoa, nutmeg, pure vanilla extract, and the original Watkins liniment. In spite of the summer heat, he wore high top black shoes with large round toes and a dark suit with a tie around the frayed collar of this white shirt. Mother always bought some cinnamon, a large bottle of vanilla to last the year, and perhaps some liniment. We all gathered in the living room to hear his sales pitch, which was delivered with great admiration for his product and a sincere sense of pride.

With the same interest he heard our family's annual news. "The Watkins Man" was the only name we children ever knew. He was more than a salesman – he was a good friend. That was the secret to his success. It was obvious that our own Watkins Man had trouble surviving on his meager commissioned salary. At the time, we, however, knew little about the immensity of the Watkins Company or the wealth that it had generated.

In Winona, Minnesota, quite far indeed from our farm, the company was established in 1868 by J. R. Watkins when he bought a buggy and began selling Dr. Ward's Vegetable Anodyne Liniment to his neighbors. His business had gown to be the oldest, largest, and most respected door-to-door sales company in the world, with 150 varieties of spices, medicines, and toilet articles. In 1911 it employed 3,000 salesmen, and by 1955 its number had grown to 15,000 with gross annual sales of 40 million dollars.

In Memphis, only 130 miles away, the company built an elaborate laboratory, office building, and warehouse to satisfy the growing demand for their products in the Southeast. Two of Mr. Watkins' stepsons moved there to run the Southern regional venture. They built a giant experimental farm to test the potential for growing exotic plants to be used in their products, such as Camphor grass from Africa, chili peppers from India, and pyrethrum flowers from Japan (which they used in their fly spray). Watkins was the largest producer of fly spray in the world. Visitors had the debatable pleasure of viewing a fly hatchery, where victims were bred for testing the power of the spray. Customers were dazzled by the sight of 100,000-gallon tanks of Watkins liniment. An added attraction for prospective customers was a racetrack with fine racehorses including Pari-mutuel, the half brother to Man o' War.

A list of the ingredients in Watkins' spices might resemble the eloquent words of a wine connoisseur, for they were made from the finest bourbon vanilla bean from Madagascar, the exceptional Tellicherry pepper from India, and the excellent Saigon cinnamon from Indochina's Cassia tree.

Heirs to the Watkins empire built their mansions in Memphis and wintered in Hawaii and Florida, but hard realities came with a faltering business and reversal of fortune. The War was to blame for the demise of the door-to-door salesmen. Women working in defense plants left no one at home to answer the door. The company's management was unwilling to move with the changing times, and the family was forced to sell.

In 1978 Irwin Jacobs bought the company and was smart enough to capitalize on the old Watkins name when he reverted to independent dealers and distributors. His strategy worked. By 1982 there were 40,000 salesmen and Fortune magazine estimated annual sales to be 50 million. To this day, 139 years from the company's inception, all a customer has to do is dial "Watkins Products" in the telephone book or look for the website, but our old friend the Watkins Man won't be there to share a meal with you and listen to your troubles and triumphs.

Morris Chapel

IT HAS BEEN there for over 100 years now. The cavernous white frame church has survived tornadoes, storms, and threats of fire, countless preachers, and inevitable financial struggles. Its steeple rises proudly on a slight ridge above the endless stretch of cultivated fields surrounding it. Crudely scratched into the concrete cornerstone are the misspelled words "Morris Chappel, 1904." My grandfather had given the church, the land, and the property across the road for a cemetery for as long as it would continue to be a place of worship. At the front of the large square building, three wooden steps lead to white painted double doors that stay locked except on the second and fourth Sabbath day. During my childhood, we never attended the services there on Sunday morning, but drove past the overflowing crowd on our way to the much smaller Methodist Church in town. When we returned on our way home again, past Morris Chapel, the service was still in motion. It sometimes lasted until 3 or 4oclock in the afternoon. Going there for Sunday service was an all day affair, especially if there was a baptism.

The large congregation was made up of not only of tenants on the Morris farm and workers from the surrounding farms, but residents of Little Rock and nearby towns. For many years, Henry Harris, my Dad's tractor driver and chief engineer for the unreliable and unpredictable machinery found in Morris Gin and most cotton gins of the time. My father depended on

Henry's faithful reliability in many things one of which was Morris Chapel. Henry had always been its chief supporter. He was in charge of the cemetery and burial grounds, keeping the preacher present and prepared for his weekly appearance and procuring the funds in the offering plate to run a church of that magnitude. Often, Henry would make a plea to my father and Uncle Lewis for some current needs of the sanctuary. My brother and I financed and Bob offered the labor of his own hands to build a back kitchen assembly room for the out of town guest who would come to this unique place of worship 2 miles from any town without food accommodations or telephone connections. It was always a mystery as to how Henry kept the sanctuary in tact, the treasury lucrative and the long wooden benches crowded to capacity.

Baptisms were held on Sunday afternoons at Clear Lake, which was another remainder of the old Arkansas Riverbed. The congregation drove, walked, or rode a wagon to the same body of water where Boy Scout outings might be held. I must have attended some swimming function there, for I remembered the terrible feeling of soft mud on the bottom squeezing between my toes.

One afternoon, my family and I stood among the crowd and waited in the background to see such a baptism. This day belonged to our cook at the time, Ossie, who walked toward the lake water in her high heels, wearing a new white crepe dress. She was led by the preacher out to waist-deep water while the congregation sang a hymn. She closed her eyes as the preacher took her in his arms and turned her backward into the water. She came up coughing and sputtering, yelling, "Yes, Lord, Yes Lord!" She triumphantly returned to shore with a broad smile on her face. The crepe dress was puckering and her shoes were muddy, but she didn't seem to notice. That next Monday morning when she came to our house, she told me that her sins had been washed away, and that she had been saved. I felt joy with her, but at my young age, I didn't know exactly what sins were or how they could be washed away in that muddy old lake, but if she was happy then I was too.

On Christmas night, we were often invited to attend the special holiday service at the sanctuary that bore our name. After supper, we put on our best clothes and drove down the road to attend the evening Christmas program. We were ushered to front row seats, directly before the pulpit. Bare light bulbs hung down from the ceiling on unadorned electrical cords. The dim illumination sent forth a candlelight glow. We sat down on hard wooden seats with the straight backs of hand-built benches made of cypress planks from the bayou. I remember feeling self-conscious, knowing that we were being watched by the entire congregation behind us. Our daddy had told us that this was a very special invitation and that we should be quiet and show them how honored we were to be there.

I later spoke with my brother and he could remember only a few details of that night. We were all very young. Perhaps it was through my parents' stories about that evening but I do recall a young woman in a white dress sitting on a bench behind the minister's pulpit with a young child beside her.

Morris Chapel

She rose to begin the service, speaking in her "company tone." On the eve of our Lord's birthday, it almost seemed fitting that we should hear the soft cry of a baby. After the first false hope that the sound from her own child would be temporary, she excused herself to attend to the child behind her.with a rather harsh whisper and then turned with great poise and a smile,, to meet the congregation and continue her Christmas message. I could not take my eyes off of the child who sat as still as a church mouse.

When it came time for collection, an usher walked up the aisle carrying a plate a basket of some kind. It was passed down all of the rows and then returned to the altar. The money was immediately counted and the exact amount was revealed. A plea began, "Could we make it an even number?" the usher asked. Again the plate was passed around on that cold night during the Great Depression.

I remember us all singing "Silent Night" together, without a hymnbook or accompaniment of any kind, but even as a child I could sense the love and the pride that they felt for their church and how pleased we were to be welcomed there. Through the years, I have attended many Christmas Eve services in churches overflowing with poinsettias, holly wreaths, velvet bows, and candlelight, while choirs sing and organs thunder forth their thrilling musical offerings to usher in the glorious Christmas Day. And yet, sometimes, I close my eyes to feel the power of those simple a cappella voices rising on that Christmas Eve once upon a time in Morris Chapel.

Today, the aging Morris Chapel is the last remnant from the past on the farm. We no longer own the land. I understand that the empty church has a roof that is in dangerous condition. The abandoned kitchen addition is now in ruins. Henry Harris is buried in the cemetery across the road with most of the tenants who once lived on our farm when I was a child. Their children and grandchildren now live in Little Rock, convenient to large modern sanctuaries., supported by affluent congregations.

I like to remember Morris Chapel with its overflowing crowd

and its choir's voices rising from to the heavens, giving so much joy to its congregations through generations. With the other noble lives that I honor from the past, Morris Chapel and its faithful congregation must certainly be among them.

Buster

IT WAS EARLY morning when the bell began to shrill against the dark winter sky. The bell did not sound to call the workers up to headquarters during the cold months of the year. My father rose quickly and hurried outside to see that Buster's house was on fire and Walter was pulling the bell rope back and forth before running back toward the burning house to help.

It was the same story. Out there that far from town, with no running water, it was impossible to fight a fire. The only course to take as the fire reached greater intensity, was to stand back and watch it take its course. I remembered the night when our barn caught on fire with all of the animals and equipment inside. The large structure (that had been there as long as my

When we still used mules

father had farmed this land) was built from cypress that my grandfather had cut and milled from the bayou. It was dry and brittle from years in the sun. There was little hope. First, all of the horses and mules were free. I watched men lined up in a row, passing down buckets of water from the nearest pump or the bayou. When they realized it was a futile effort, their shouts died down to a sudden silence while the cracking and falling of timbers echoed in the night. The next morning we stood among the ruins and smoldering ashes while my father quietly surveyed how he would start all over again.

This morning was different. Buster's daughter and her two babies were inside the house. Buster had come from his own house when he noticed the blaze and called to his daughter as he ran up the steps. No one answered and he ran through the door of the dry cypress shack and into the fire. He managed to pull out his daughter, who held a tiny baby, grab "Junebug," his toddling grandson, and pull them outside. His arms and hands were burned and so was Junebug's face. His daughter lay quiet and still on the grass, clinging to her child. My father ran for the car, lay Buster's daughter on the back seat with the baby, and put Buster with Junebug on his lap. Buster cradled the sobbing boy with a rocking motions and whispered to him that everything would be all right. That Sunday Buster came home triumphantly with Junebug. When the bandages were removed, the boy's face was distorted and pulled to one side by the cruel heat. But there was something about Junebug's smile that turned the horror of that morning into joy. He was a living tribute to Buster's bravery and partial victory. Buster and Mattie raised him in their old age and he was the happy grandchild who took care of them in their later years.

Walter Bell

WE CALLED WALTER Bell "the hostler." He caught my father's horse and had it hitched up at the gate for him every morning for his daily surveillance of the farm. He helped my brother Billy up on his Pinto pony, and was never too busy to saddle a horse for me when I came home from school. Walter saw that the horses were fed, combed, shod, and ready to ride at all times. He really had a way with animals. He could go out into an open pasture and "talk" the horse right into the bridle. He showed me how he stood in the pasture without looking too anxious. I watched him approach the horse with the bridle behind his back, walking slowly toward him talking all of the time, looking right in his eye. When he was close enough, he reached out for his mane, and gently slipped the bridle over his nose. Walter could quiet the meanest of our horses and ride those that seemed impossible to train.

Once, my father bought cattle. That was the new way to make money and use untillable land for pasture. It only lasted for a while, for I suppose being a cattle farmer is "in your blood" just as it was in the cowboy movies. Dad was no cattle farmer. At any rate, when his enthusiasm was at its peak, he acquired several quarter horses to drive the cattle whenever they needed to be moved. Walter could "turn his horse on a dime" and taught his fellow workers how to accomplish the task. This is how we came by the few horses that remained.

Walter took care of the mules also. He would have liked to do all of the plowing with mules, even after my father purchased a steel-wheeled tractor during the '30s. He understood the mules. He had carefully written each of their names in their designated stall in the barn and talked with them each morning. It was Walter who mated them for plough teams. Pairing properly was important because mismatched mules would fight and day's work would be spoiled.

Walter never got used to anything mechanical. Mowing the big front yard was part of his chore each week. He hated it almost as much as driving a tractor. When he was forced into the task by necessity, Walter conscientiously stuck out his hand to signal for a left-hand turn as he came to the end of a row in the plowed field. Walter was tall and skinny with almost no shape for his clothes to hang on to. A long neck extended from his thin, sloping shoulders and supported a head that seemed almost too small for his body. Perched on the thin short wool covering his head was an old faded blue and white railroad cap.

Walter lived right beside the pasture with his heavyset wife, Lula Bell. They had no children. We never used her up at the house because Mama said she couldn't cook. Mama always seemed to know about those things. Lula was the slowest chopper and cotton picker there was on the place, but she loved Walter.

He came to our door every Christmas morning, grinning as his deep raspy voice yelled with joy, "Christmas Gift!"

Daddy rode a tall, sorrel Tennessee Walker with a handsome flowing mane. Together they seemed to perform a graceful dance as he pranced down the turn rows, carrying my father who sat tall and proud rocking with the smooth rhythm of his horse. When I rode beside him, I urged my horse to a faster pace in order to catch up with them, holding him in a smooth single-foot gait as I had been taught.

Then there were the moonlight rides for Walter to endure. My older

Dad with his favorite "walker."

brother invited his high school friends out in the summer to go riding after dark. There was something glamorous about riding horses at night. When there was a full moon, it was bright enough to see everything around us. The girls arrived giggling and most did not know how to ride. My brother was quite patient with them for some reason. The boys were careless and knew nothing about the feelings of our horses. I could see Walter Bell eyeing them suspiciously as he patiently helped each one on a horse.

It was exciting to ride in the cool night down a dusty road turned to silver in the moonlight. The white cotton blossoms, illuminated in the celestial glow, changed the dusty noonday fields into gigantic flower gardens. Bob took more chances, urging his horse to go faster and leaping across the ditches in a dramatic fashion, showing off for the girls. In the end, we always came home to Walter, who was waiting up to unsaddle his charges and turn them out to pasture.

Riding was a big part of my life growing up, and Walter was always there to teach me and help me learn how to care for the horses that I rode. I miss him, and with him, I miss the sense of independence and freedom that came with galloping across a field where I could feel and smell the change of the seasons in the rush of wind on my face. During those rides I was a part of the earth and all its miracles and so was Walter Bell.

Leaving Home

ONE SEPTEMBER MORNING when I was 15, my parents drove me away from the bayou. By now the price of cotton had risen to 40 cents a pound and Aaron had his own car. The autumn day was cool, bringing a sadness that always tugged at me when summer was over. In the back of the car was a large metal trunk filled with clothes purchased from Little Rock stores. I was feeling self-conscious in my first high heels and a brand new dark cotton suit. We headed toward the overnight train that would take me to Ward Belmont, a girl's boarding school in Nashville. Taking one last look at the bayou, I saw the leaves were turning yellow. I sensed that this would be the end of walking barefoot in the velvet dust and feeling more freedom than I would ever experience again.

I would come home often on holidays and summer break, but I would never live there again permanently. Through the years, I watched the changes on the farm. More and more, the few tenants remaining would go to town and find jobs there. Cleve landed a job with a railroad company as a distinguished steward on the train to New Orleans. The tenant houses that long ago dotted the terrain disappeared with that entire system of life. Cotton was no longer the crop. The leveled land was efficiently turned by massive equipment that prepared the soil for endless rows of soybeans, wheat and rice patties from a country far away. The vast fields were unobstructed by the cluttered yards, woodpiles, and porches of the families that once lived there.

During my sophomore year in college, 1951-52, my father built Mama her dream home in Keo. When the handsome Williamsburg Colonial structure with white columns rose from the pecan orchard, Dad couldn't get her to move there. She kept begging, "just one more night at home, William." But "time heals all" and soon my parents began to enjoy their new home in town for several well-earned years of retirement. Mama had my wedding reception there and I walked down the stairwell, designed for that occasion.

Mother's dream house

After I married and moved to Memphis, we often drove our three children back to Keo and the bayou for Thanksgiving or Christmas. They were delighted with the wonders that they found there. At first there was riding in my Dad's pony cart and then they graduated to riding horses and land vehicles on the farm. My brother, Bob and his family lived in Keo next door to their grandparents. His three boys and daughter attended school in Little Rock. During those early years the cousins took my children over to the stores in town. They were amazed that they could just walk a short distance across the railroad track, to get there. It had changed very little in all of that time except that Mr. Leake was gone. It was remarkable that my children were able to meet some of the people I had known there in my childhood.

In her fine new home, my mother continued to cook her own turkey and her exceptional cornbread dressing each year but now it was baked in the latest Thermador oven and sliced with an electric knife. She spread the miracles of her modern kitchen on her dining table and my children witnessed her magic. Her last years were glorious ones. Her remarkable influence on my children was apparent. Each time I went to Atlanta, where they all lived, I found strong evidence that they had inherited Mama's ability to bring the same enchantment to their tables in their own homes to a new generation.

But time was running out. My parents had to move into a retirement community when Dad succumbed to the ravages of a sudden stroke that left him helpless for five years. Mama and Billy settled into an apartment in Little Rock where they visited Dad every single day and continued to find miracles as long as they lived.

Thanksgiving dinner in Keo

The Land

ONCE, I SAT with my father in his small dusty office in the cotton gin. He pointed to a worn map of Lonoke County on the wall behind his desk. The family names of the landowners were emblazoned on the thick fabric of the aged and worn depiction of farms surrounding our land. Some still owned thousands of acres that their family had handed down to them. Others had lost it all. My father looked me straight in the eye and said, "Remember this, if you don't remember another thing: hang onto the land. There's always someone standing in line to take it away from you. God doesn't make any more of it!" I watched his eyes shine with the sudden surge of pride in owning land.

Somewhere on the Internet in that vast source of information found there, I ran across the letters of J. Hector St. John de Crevecoeur, published in 1882. This French emigrant, turned American farmer, expressed the same exhilaration in land ownership:

> "I never return home without feeling pleasing emotion…
> the instant I enter on our land, the bright idea of property
> of exclusive right, of independence, exalt my mind. Precious
> soil, I say to myself…no wonder that we should thus cherish
> its possession, no wonder that so many Europeans, who have
> never been able to say that such portion of land was theirs,

cross the Atlantic to realize that happiness. The formerly rude soil has been converted by my father into a pleasant farm and in return, it has established all our rights: on it is founded our rank, our freedom, our powers as citizens, our importance as inhabitants of such a district. These images, I must confess, I always behold with pleasure and extend them as far as my imagination can reach."

During the years after my father died, my brothers and I remained faithful stewards of the land. My father had five grandsons but my brother's oldest child, Michael, was the only one who inherited his grandfather's innate love of farming. With the same devotion and reverence, he began to work the land as a renter. For several years, he owned the farm and continued to plow the fields that belonged to his great-great-grandfather. But after years of holding fast to my father's wishes, my nephew struggled with the maze of farm subsidies, government control, and the unreliable forces of nature. He knew it was impossible for a small farm to survive and he knew he must sell.

A physician from the Northwest bought our land as an investment. It was difficult to imagine our beloved land as a mere investment. The new owner might never know the history, the victories, the hearts and souls of the families that once lived there. But in all of our discouragement and heartache over the loss of our land, we found another miracle... my nephew was able to retain ownership of the bayou. The aerial photograph of the Morris Brake that carries our family name, hangs in my kitchen. I can see it encircling the land where we once lived. I find comfort in that.

The two and one half hour drive from Memphis gets longer as we age, but the bayou remains unchanged. Its cypress trees are taller and thicker with their branches hanging over the seldom-traveled road.

Most of the people in my stories are gone now. Their disappointments and triumphs have been plowed under by time, covered over in the eternal cycle of new generations. Children and grandchildren have moved into town and cities. Memories grow dim but the stories of the noble lives that were so much a part of my childhood have been kept as new as a spring rain in my heart and on the pages of this lifelong endeavor.

Michael and Sissy at the bayou